MW01118518

The Peter Bedrick Young People's Encyclopedia

History of the World

The Editors of Larousse

PETER BEDRICK BOOKS
NTC/Contemporary Publishing Group

Library of Congress
Cataloging-in-Publication Data
History of the world / the editors of Larousse.
p. cm. (The Peter Bedrick young people's encyclopedia)
Originally published: France : Larousse-Bordas, 1996.
ISBN 0-87226-626-5
1. World history—Encyclopedias, Juvenile. I. Larousse (Firm) II. Title.
D21.H754 2000
903—dc21 00-45515
CIP

This volume forms part of the Young People's Encyclopedia. It was produced under the editorial direction of Claude Naudin, Marie-Lise Cuq and Anne Luthaud. Text contributors: Anne-Marie Lelorrain, Philippe Brochard, Annie Forgeau, Laurence Massénat and Catherine Salles, assisted by Bénédicte Houdré and Olivier Cornu.

Graphic design and art direction by Anne Boyer, assisted by Emmanuel Chaspoul
Layout by Laure Massin
Technical coordination by Pierre Taillemite
Proofreading, revision by Annick Valade, assisted by Monique Bagaïni and Françoise Moulard
Picture editing by Anne-Marie Moyse-Jaubert
Picture research by Nathalie Lassaire
Production by Annie Botrel
Cover by Gérard Fritsch, assisted by Véronique Laporte

English translation by Donald Gecewicz

Consultant in Canada
Ariane Archambault
Acknowledgments to M. Henri Bulawko vice-president of CRIF

First published in the United States in 2001 by Peter Bedrick Books
A division of NTC/Contemporary Publishing Group, Inc.
4255 West Touhy Avenue, Lincolnwood (Chicago), Illinois 60712-1975 U.S.A.

Printed in France
International Standard Book Number: 0-87226-626-5

01 02 03 04 8 7 6 5 4 3 2 1

Discovering the Yo

History of the World

From prehistory to our own time, this volume describes the great events in the history of the world.

How to use this book

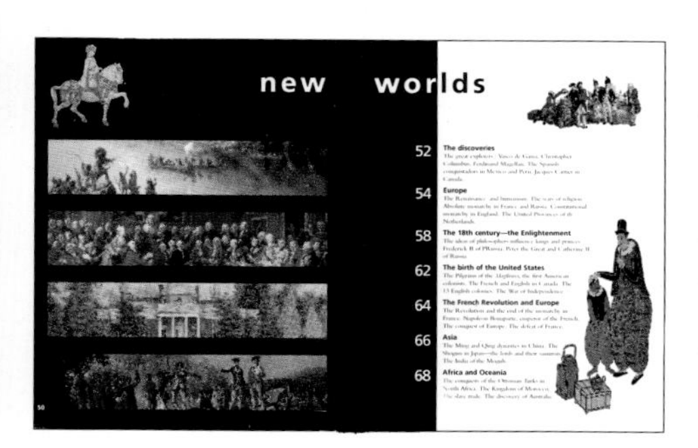

This volume is divided into five parts. Each part is introduced by an outline listing the various chapters and giving a short summary of their content.

Each part deals with one of the major periods of world history in Europe, America, Asia, Africa and Oceania.

Large double-page photographs illustrate key historical moments from ancient times to the present.

At the end of the volume, a timeline of history makes it possible to compare the history of different countries at any given period.

An index gives quick page reference for the particular information you are looking for.

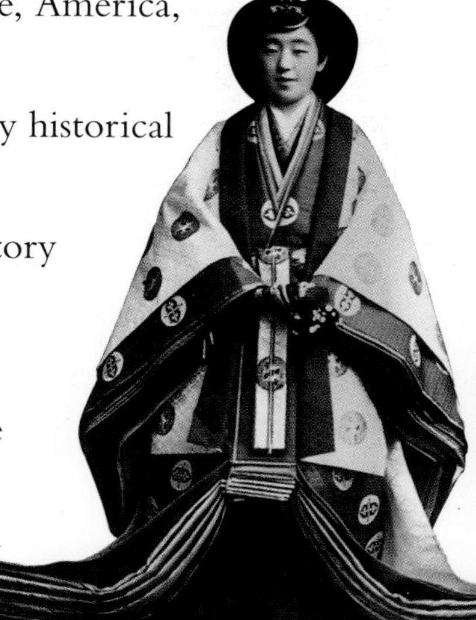

g People's Encyclopedia

chapter title
Each chapter unfolds over one or two double-page spreads.

introductory text
At the beginning of each chapter there is a summary of the subject to be described in the following pages.

panoramic photograph
This illustrates one of the topics of the chapter.

marginal texts
These contain additional information.

The United States as the world's leading power exercises influence over many countries in Latin America. The states of Latin America are making efforts to assert their independence from their powerful neighbor.

The Americas

- **1946** Argentina: Juan Perón is elected president.
- **1950-1954** United States: Senator Joseph McCarthy leads a campaign against communists.
- **1959** Cuba: Fidel Castro takes power.
- **1963** August, United States: march by blacks on Washington.
- **1963** November, United States: assassination of John F. Kennedy in Dallas.
- **1968** United States: assassination of Martin Luther King in Memphis.
- **1969** Two Americans walk on the moon.
- **1973** Chile: Allende is overthrown by the dictator Pinochet.
- **1982** Canada: the constitution becomes a solely Canadian responsibility.
- **1983** Argentina: end of the military dictatorship, Raul Alfonsín becomes president.
- **1991** The United States leads the allies in the Gulf War.

Since 1945, the United States has maintained its position as the leading world power. Canada, in the north of the American continent, broke its last constitutional link with Britain in the 1980s.

The United States, a world power

The United States has powerful armed forces and weapons and vast financial resources, and has made great technological advances in aviation, shipping and industry. It is a rich country, wielding influence over a large part of the world. The American way of life has become a model for many people: for example, high-rise cities and a wide range of consumer goods (products used in daily life). As leader of the Western bloc (see p. 100-101), the United States worked to prevent communism from spreading abroad and within its frontiers. From 1950 to 1954, under presidents Truman and Eisenhower, Senator Joseph McCarthy led a national campaign against communists. Elected president in 1960, the Democrat John F. Kennedy sought to give his country a new boost and proposed two major objectives: greater social justice and the conquest of space. He was assassinated in 1963. In 1969, two American astronauts, Neil Armstrong and Edwin Aldrin, walked on the moon.

John F. Kennedy and his wife in New York during the 1960 election campaign. ▼

Difficult years

The southern states of the USA practiced racial segregation – ogranized and regulated separation of blacks and whites in schools and public places. From 1955, the black Baptist minister Martin Luther King Jr. campaigned for civil rights for black Americans. In 1957, riots broke out in Little Rock, in Arkansas, during desegregation of the schools. In 1963, with support from President Kennedy, several thousand blacks ogranized a march on Washington. A civil-rights law guaranteeing a number of rights to blacks was passed in 1964. However, protests continued. The Black Muslim leader Malcolm X was assassinated in 1965 and Martin Luther King in 1968. In the 1960s, student protest movements rose up against mainstream American society that to some seemed based on money and consumption. Students also opposed the sending of troops to Vietnam (see p. 105). Increasing numbers of other Americans denounced this war as unjustified. In 1973, under President Richard Nixon, the Americans withdrew from Vietnam. The Vietnam War, in which 50,000 U.S. soldiers died and tens of thousands were wounded, had traumatized the country.

110

Skyscrapers of Manhattan, New York City.

Martin Luther King in 1963.

The United States today

In the 1970s, disarmament talks were started with the USSR. At the same period, the United States went through a serious crisis linked to the rise in the price of oil (see p. 107). In 1974, the Watergate scandal broke when the Republican president, Nixon, was accused of knowing about an illegal entry into the Watergate building, headquarters of the Democratic party. Nixon was forced to resign. In the 1980s, under Ronald Reagan's presidency, the number of unemployed and poor increased, as in many other developed countries. In industry, the Japanese competed successfully with the Americans, especially in the car and computer sectors. However, the U.S. economy recovered, and at the turn of the millennium, the United States is still the world's richest and most powerful state.

Canada

From 1948, Canada began to develop a policy of alignment with the United States. In 1982, it broke the last official link with Great Britain: from then on its constitution was alterable only by the Canadian government. Canada is made up of ten provinces and two territories. The central government exercises authority over the provinces, which have their own governments, which tend to seek more power and money to apply their own programs. Quebec, the only majority French-speaking province of Canada, has a separatist movement demanding d unique status and even independence. The American Indians and the Inuit (the country's original inhabitants) want greater respect for their ancestral rights and more autonomy. □

Vancouver, a great Canadian city ▲

Vancouver, in the province of British Columbia, is Canada's third city, with more than 1.4 million inhabitants. Founded at the end of the 19th century, it is a modern city with a distinctive style of architecture. It owes its rapid growth to the railway and its privleged position on the Pacific Ocean, which makes it the country's leading port.

◄ The American software magnate, Bill Gates.

111

time line
The dates of important events are given here.

heading
Each subsection expands on a basic aspect of the subject.

photo caption
This explains the illustration.

Cont

e n t s

th

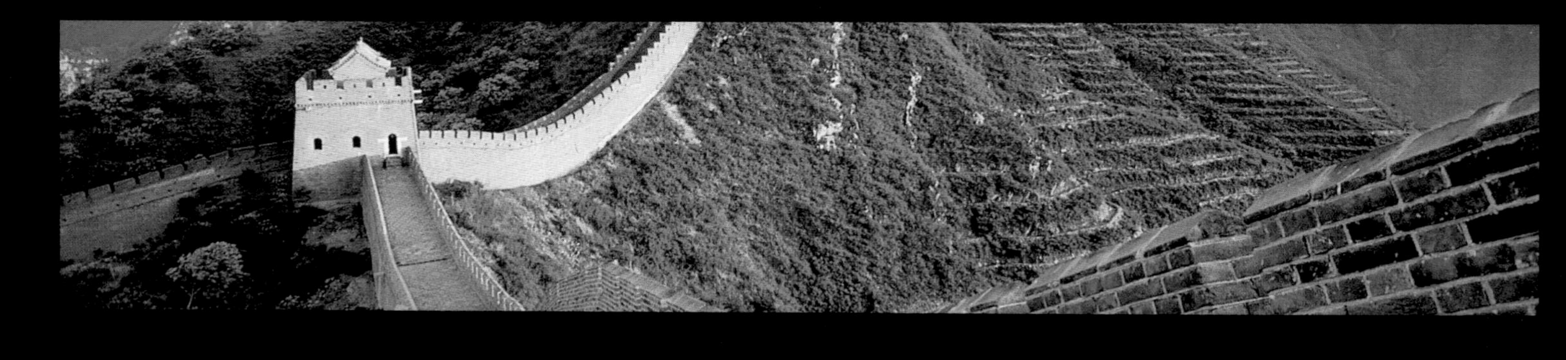

first civilizations

Prehistory describes the time from the emergence of our earliest ancestors—over 6 million years ago—to the invention of writing around 3100 BC, which marks the beginning of history.

Prehistory

BC

6,000,000 First hominids in Africa.
3,500,000 First australopithecines in Africa.
2,500,000 First *Homo habilis* in Africa; manufacture of first tools.
1,500,000 First *Homo erectus* in Africa, last australopithecines, last *Homo habilis*.
900,000 Migrations of *Homo erectus* from Africa to western Asia, Indonesia and China.
500,000 *Homo erectus* masters fire.
100,000 First *Homo sapiens*; working of flint.
40,000 First *Homo sapiens sapiens*.
35,000 The world population reaches 4 million.
30,000 Migrations of *Homo sapiens sapiens* from Europe and Asia to Australia and America.
10,000 The world population reaches 7 million.
8000 Beginning of the Neolithic period in the Middle East; first agriculture.
6500 Building of first towns in the Middle East.
5500 Manufacture of copper.
5000 The world population reaches 50 million.
3100 Invention of writing, manufacture of bronze.

Our most distant ancestors, the hominids, were not completely human. Paleontologists, who specialize in studying prehistory, think that they appeared more than 6 million years ago on the African continent. However, the first remains so far discovered date from about 3.5 million years ago. The first humans lived mainly by hunting and gathering. As they evolved, they migrated toward new continents. Then they began to build settlements, raise animals and grow crops.

The first human beings populate the Earth

The first period of prehistory, known as the Paleolithic, lasted almost 3 million years. During this time, people lived by fishing, hunting and gathering. In this period, too, they made the first tools. Human evolution was very gradual. The earliest hominid remains have been discovered in East Africa. They are the bones of "Lucy," a female who probably lived about 3.5 million years ago. She was one of the hominids called australopithecines, so named because their bones were found in southern Africa. "Abel," whose jawbones were found in central Africa, dates from around the same period. Southern Africa was also the home, 2.5 million years ago, of people called *Homo habilis* ("skillful man"), so named because they knew how to make stone tools and build huts. *Homo habilis* lived at the same time as the last australopithecines, but it is not known whether these human ancestors evolved from the australopithecines or developed in parallel. Then, about 1.5 million years ago, *Homo erectus* ("upright man") emerged. These were the first hominids to stand completely upright. By 500,000 years ago, people knew how to make fire. *Homo habilis* and another species, *Homo erectus*, evolved, but gradually became extinct. Around 100,000 years ago, *Homo sapiens* ("wise man") appeared, with the ability to make increasingly complex tools. Finally, 40,000 years ago appeared *Homo sapiens sapiens*, the prehistoric humans closest to modern people. These people were nomads, moving from place to place and setting up huts or tents when they changed hunting territory. They knew how to make blades from flint. With bone needles and animal sinews, they sewed together skins to make clothes and canoes. Around 20,000 years ago, they painted the walls of caves, which were probably sacred sites.

The first migrations

Throughout their evolution, humans migrated. It seems that about 900,000 years ago, a number of the species *Homo erectus* left Africa to settle in Western Asia and later in Indonesia and China. By

Bifacial ▶ flint tool, 100,000 years old.

Harpoon ▶ made of reindeer antler.

Cave painting found in the Sahara Desert at Tassili.

850,000 years ago, some had found their way to Europe. At this time, America and Oceania (Australia and the Pacific islands) were still uninhabited. *Homo sapiens* developed in Europe and Asia before settling in Australia. Finally, around 30,000 years ago, *Homo sapiens* passed from Asia to America across the Bering Strait. The island groups of the Pacific Ocean were not populated until 2000 BC and New Zealand as late as AD 1000.

The first farmers, the first towns

People began to rely less and less on hunting. They became settled, staying in specific regions of the continents where they lived. Society changed. People gathered in groups and built houses of clay and straw. They raised animals and then grew crops. In this way, agriculture began. This second and last period of prehistory, the Neolithic, lasted from about 8000 BC to about 3000 BC. As with the Paleolithic, it did not come to an end everywhere at the same time, since technical developments did not take place on all the continents simultaneously. The first evidence of farming has been found in the Middle East, in what is now Iraq. Farmers were growing wheat in this region around 8000 BC. At the same time, Africans were cultivating millet, and Europeans lentils and peas. Thanks to the advances in agriculture, living conditions improved: food was more plentiful and people lived longer. The world's population increased. The first towns, Jericho (modern Palestine) and Çatalhüyük (modern Turkey), were built in the Middle East around 6500 BC. Neolithic people specialized. Some made pottery. Others made baskets, fabrics and jewelry. Smiths worked metals. People were ranked in society according to their trades and their influence. As money did not yet exist, trade was by barter (exchange) of food and articles. People wanted to make lists of what belonged to whom and to keep records of trading operations. Around 3100 BC, writing was invented. This marked the beginning of history. □

A sling, or catapult, used by a hunter about 13,000 BC. ▼

Terra-cotta statue of a seated woman, made around the 6th century BC and found in Serbia. ▼

Skull of an australopithecus

Pictured below is a hominid more than 3 million years old. It had a heavy, protruding jaw. Its teeth were larger than

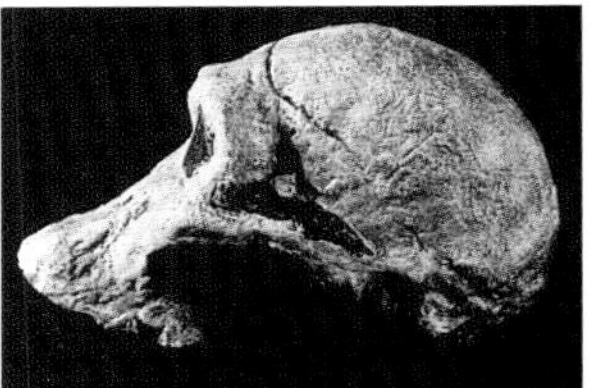

ours. Its forehead receded and a bony brow jutted out above its eyes. The cranial capacity of the australopithecines was small: less than 500 cm³ (30 cubic inches). Ours is 1500 cm³ (90 cubic inches), so their brain was smaller in comparison. Study of australopithecine skeletons shows that they moved about on two legs and also jumped from tree to tree. They were between 1.10 m and 1.40 m (3.5 to 4.5 ft) tall. *Homo habilis*, who lived 2.5 million years ago, was larger and had a larger skull and a smaller arch over the eyes than the australopithecines.

One of the world's oldest civilizations emerged in Mesopotamia, between the rivers Tigris and Euphrates. In the region of Sumer, around 3100 BC, the first written texts appeared.

Mesopotamia

BC

3100 Invention of cuneiform script in Sumer.
2800 Emergence of the first city-states of Sumer.
2300 Sargon, king of Akkad, founds an empire.
2100 Invasion of the Amorites and fall of the city of Ur.
1792-1750 Hammurabi, an Amorite king, becomes king of Babylon.
1595 Invasion of the Babylonian empire by the Hittites.
1390 Beginning of Assyrian expansion.
1235 Capture of Babylon by the Assyrians.
612 Capture of Nineveh, the Assyrian capital, by the Babylonians; Babylon becomes the capital of an empire again.
605-562 New Babylonian empire: Nebuchadnezzar II, king of Babylon.
539 The Persians occupy Babylon.

Mesopotamia (from the Greek word meaning "the land between the rivers") was a vast fertile region that lay in what are today Iraq and Syria. Akkad, the center of this region, was occupied from 3500 BC by the Semites, who came originally from the northwest. At Sumer in the south, near the Persian Gulf, a people settled of whose origins we know little—the Sumerians. Around 2800 BC, the Sumerians began to build towns that became city-states, each with its own god and its own laws. The Sumerians were invaded by various peoples, including the Akkadians, who founded their own empires. These empires disappeared in 539 BC, when Mesopotamia was conquered by the Persians, who came from the area that is modern Iran.

The development of writing in Sumer

In the region of Sumer, archeologists have found clay tablets engraved with wedge-shaped signs dating from 3100 BC. These signs were impressed on clay with pointed reeds and the clay was then baked. Each sign represents a sound or a syllable, and they form one of the oldest known scripts, called "cuneiform" (from the Latin *cuneus*, meaning "wedge"). It is thought that these tablets were first used to keep the accounts of Sumerian merchants. Later, this script spread throughout all Mesopotamia, and much of what we know about the organization of the city-states comes from such texts. Each state was ruled by a king who was thought to represent the city's god. Some of the city-states, especially Ur, became very powerful and dominated the others, but gradually the cities of Sumer became weaker. They were invaded by the armies of King Sargon who, from his base in Akkad, founded the first empire in this region about 2300 BC. Then, around 2100 BC, new conquerors overran Mesopotamia, and the city-states disappeared completely. Around 1792 BC, Hammurabi was the first ruler to unify the region. He established his capital at Babylon, in the south of Mesopotamia, and created the first Babylonian empire.

A temple attendant, dressed in a woolen robe, from the 3rd millennium BC. ▼

Hammurabi's code

King Hammurabi is famous for what is known as the Code of Hammurabi, a body of laws that the king had drawn up and engraved on stone near the end of his reign. These written laws applied to all the peoples of the Babylonian empire, while the old Sumerian city-states had each had their own laws. Hammurabi's code laid down rules for both public life within the empire and the private life of each individual. However, the king's laws had little time to have effect. After the king's death, the empire weakened, and

A dinner for important people in the city of Ur.

Assyrian king hunting lions, a 9th-century BC bas-relief from the palace of Nimrud. ▼

in 1595 BC, it was invaded by the Hittites from Asia Minor. Mesopotamia was again split into different states. Not until 1390 BC did a new empire arise, that of the Assyrians.

The Assyrian empire

Assyria was in the north of Mesopotamia. In the 14th century BC, it was a warrior state governed by a monarch wielding absolute power. The Assyrians were conquerors. They seized the lands bordering the Mediterranean and then, in 1235 BC, the Babylonian empire. The Assyrians formed a new empire with its capital at Nineveh in the north of Mesopotamia. However, in 612 BC the Babylonians rebelled and seized Nineveh. This was the end of the Assyrian empire. Freed of Assyrian domination, a second Babylonian empire emerged with Babylon once again its capital.

The renaissance of Babylon

The most powerful king of the new Babylonian empire was Nebuchadnezzar II. He extended the empire's territory and conquered the city of Jerusalem, deporting thousands of Hebrews to Babylon. In Babylon he had extraordinary "hanging gardens" built in tiered terraces and tended by slaves who brought up water from the Euphrates. The gardens, which no longer exist, were one of the Seven Wonders of the ancient world. Babylon's empire was threatened from the east by the Persians. Their king Cyrus captured Babylon in 539 BC and so ended the last of the Mesopotamian empires. □

Mesopotamia

Mesopotamia was only rarely unified. It was by turns dominated by the cities of the south (Ur, Babylon) or by the Assyrians from the north. ▼

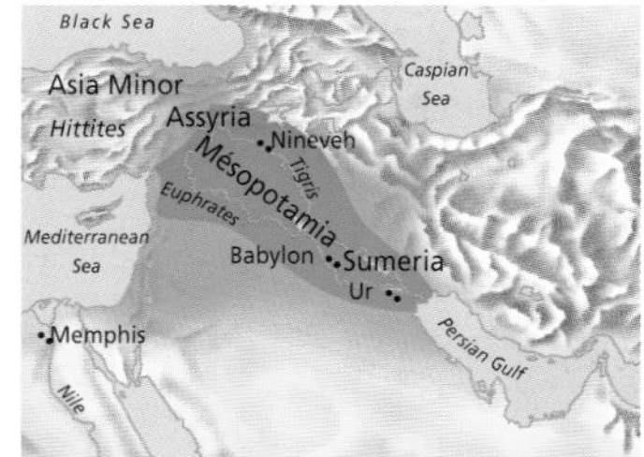

The Hebrews

The Hebrews were the first people to worship only one god. Beginning as nomads, they were eventually conquered by Egypt. Around 1200 BC they established an independent nation in Palestine, governed first by Saul and later by David and his son Solomon. Later they were again conquered, first by the Assyrians and then by the Babylonians.▼

Egyptian civilization developed along the Nile, between North Africa and Asia Minor. Around 3100 BC, the Egyptians invented hieroglyphics, one of the world's first writing systems.

Egypt

BC

c. 3100 First hieroglyphics. The first pharaoh, Menes, unifies the country.
2660-2180 Old Kingdom (3rd-6th dynasties. Pharaohs Cheops, Khephren, Mykerinos).
2180-2060 First Intermediate Period (7th-10th dynasties).
2060-1650 Middle Kingdom (11th-13th dynasties. Pharaohs Sesostris I, II, III).
1650-1530 Second Intermediate Period (14th-17th dynasties).
1530-1069 New Kingdom (18th-20th dynasties. Pharaohs Amenhotep IV, Tutankhamun, Ramses II).
1069-664 Third Intermediate Period.
664 Beginning of the Late Period (Sais pharaohs).
525 Persian domination.
332 Alexander the Great conquers Egypt.
323 Beginning of Greek period: dynasty of the Ptolemies.
30 Egypt becomes a Roman province.

Egyptian peasant plowing a field, from a New Kingdom tomb, 1300 BC.

Egypt, crossed by the Nile River, is a long oasis hemmed in between two desert plateaus. Each year, the regular flooding of the river washes over and fertilizes its banks. The country was unified for the first time about 3100 BC under the rule of a king, the pharaoh. The pharaoh was a sacred figure who governed the country with the aid of scribes, who alone had knowledge of writing, and priests, who honored the numerous gods. The vast majority of the people were farmers. The history of ancient Egypt lasted some 3000 years.

◀ A baker at work.

A long history

Egyptian history is split into three chief periods known as "kingdoms," which date from around 2660 to 1069 BC. During the Old Kingdom, the capital was at Memphis. During the Middle and New Kingdoms, there were several royal residences, the most important being Thebes. The kingdoms were periods of stability and prosperity. In between occurred times of unrest, the "intermediate periods." At the end of the Third Intermediate Period in 664 BC came the Late Period that ended in 332 BC when Alexander, king of Macedonia, conquered Egypt. The pharaohs are grouped into thirty dynasties, from the first pharaoh until the conquest by Alexander. Egypt was then governed by Greek kings, the Ptolemies, who made Alexandria their capital. Queen Cleopatra VII was the last of the Ptolemies to rule in Egypt before the Romans occupied the country.

Hieroglyphics, the writing of the Egyptians.

The pharaoh

The word "pharaoh" comes from the Egyptian *per-aa*, which first meant "great house" (the palace and its administration) before it came to designate the king. The Egyptians considered the pharaoh to be the human representative of the gods. He therefore shared with the numerous Egyptian gods (see *Religions of the World*) the ownership of the earth and the riches of the soil. He was all-powerful, the chief priest and the person who decided on peace or war. To the Egyptians, when the pharaoh conquered territories, he had extended the limits of the world that the gods had created. After his death, the pharaoh's body was mummified, together with the bodies of his servants: it was embalmed and wrapped in linen bandages and then placed in a coffin. The Egyptians believed that mummification made it possible for the pharaoh to rejoin the world of the gods. During the Old and Middle Kingdoms, pharaohs such as Cheops built pyramids—stone tombs more than 100 m (390 ft) in height. The pyramids represent immense sun rays that were to assist the pharoah's ascent into the heavens. Pharaohs of the New Kingdom, such as the queen Hatshepsut (1520-1484 BC) and king Tutankhamun (1354-1346 BC), were buried in underground tombs hollowed out on the left bank of the Nile at a site known as the Valley of the Kings.

Society

We know about the daily lives of the Egyptians from the objects buried with them and from the scenes engraved and painted on the walls of their tombs. The life of Egyptian peasants revolved around the annual flooding of the Nile. After the flood, they sowed and harvested. While they waited for the next flood, they did building work for the pharaoh. Temples, houses and brick palaces were built outside the crop-growing lands. The learned class, the scribes, played an important part: some were concerned with taxes and administration, while others drew up religious texts. The scribes wrote in hieroglyphics, a sacred script that used drawings to represent objects, actions or sounds. Hieroglyphics is one of the first known writing systems. The priests were guardians of the magnificent temples and responsible for the worship of the many gods. During the Old and Middle Kingdoms, the pharaohs recruited their army from the people. In the New Kingdom, wars became more frequent and the pharaohs paid soldiers to fight. Conquest brought substantial riches to the country, in the form of booty and tributes paid by subject peoples. However, in the 7th century BC, Egypt began to decline. The country suffered a series of invasions by the Assyrians, the Persians and the Greeks. In 30 BC, the Romans conquered Egypt, and it became a Roman province. □

Pharaoh Amenhotep II (1450-1425 BC). ►

Queen Hatshepsut

Despite the small false beard that she wore like other pharaohs, Hatshepsut was a woman. Daughter, wife and half-sister of pharaohs, she reigned in the 15th century BC.

Queen Nefertiti

Wife of the pharaoh Akhenaton (1372-1354 BC), Nefertiti is famed for her beauty. She seems to have played an important role in the reforms of her husband, who established the worship of a single god, the sun god Aton. ▼

The first area of India to be settled was the north, between the Indus River, which gives its name to the country, and the Ganges River. There, a civilization as ancient as those of Mesopotamia and Egypt arose.

India

BC

c. 7000 Building of the first villages in northern India.
2400 Construction of the first cities, including Mohenjo-Daro and Harappa.
1500 Disappearance of the Indus civilization, invasion of the Aryans.
560-480 Life of the Buddha.
519-512 Conquest of the north of India by the Persian king Darius.
450 The Aryan civilization reaches southern India.
327-325 Conquest of the north of India by the Greeks led by Alexander.
320 Foundation of the Maurya dynasty, the first great Indian dynasty.
269 Accession of the Maurya king, Asoka.
232 Death of Asoka.
185 Overthrow of the Maurya dynasty; division of India into small kingdoms.

AD

1st-2nd c. Invasion of northern India by the Kushan people, foundation of the Kushan empire.
4th c. King Chandragupta I founds the Gupta dynasty.
5th c. Invasion of the Huns in the northwest of India. End of the Gupta dynasty.

Ancient India covered the territories of modern India, Pakistan and Bangladesh. Several civilizations evolved there but without ever dominating the whole area, which is so vast that it is often referred to as "the Indian subcontinent." Regularly invaded from the north, India rarely formed a unified empire in ancient times. Only two dynasties, the Maurya and later the Gupta, extended their rule over almost the whole country.

The cities of the Indus

The first Indians, who were probably the Dravidians, established villages in the north of ancient India (modern Pakistan) from 7000 BC. These people were herdsmen and skillful artisans, using potter's wheels and making ceramics. Around 2400 BC, they built large walled cities, among them Mohenjo-Daro and Harappa. These were probably designed by planners who were specialists in constructing cities. Their brick buildings lined straight streets that intersected at right angles in a grid pattern. A highly developed system of channels ensured a supply of running water. From excavations carried out in these towns, we are quite well-informed about the life of their people. We know that they traded with Mesopotamia and used a writing system. However, the reasons why the Indus civilization disappeared about 1500 BC are unknown.

Bust of a priest-king ▲ from the city of Mohenjo-Daro, about 2400-2200 BC.

The Aryans and the caste system

At the time that the Indus civilization disappeared, peoples from Persia (modern Iran) known as the Aryans invaded the north of India and settled there. These peoples, who were lighter-skinned than the Dravidians, brought with them a civilization that was gradually adopted by most of the peoples of India. The Dravidians have, however, remained the majority in the south of India to the present day. The Aryans spoke Sanskrit, the language in which their sacred texts, the Vedas, are written. These texts are the basis of their religion, Hinduism, which is still practiced in India (see *Religions of the World*). The Aryans also introduced the system of dividing society into castes. Each person is born into a caste, a closed social group that it is impossible to leave. There are more than one hundred castes, corresponding to professions, and they can be grouped in four categories: the *brahmans*,who pray and teach, the soldier caste of the *kshatriya*, and the *vaisya* and *sudra* who perform manual work. People who do not belong to any of these castes are considered impure. They are called "pariahs" or "untouchables" and are entitled only to perform work rejected by the others. For more than a thousand years, the Aryans extended their dominion south and west but they could not resist the arrival of new conquerors from the north.

The empire of Asoka

The north of India was conquered by the Persian king Darius in the 6th century BC and then by the Greek army of Alexander

Elephants sculpted on a Buddhist monument of the 2nd century BC.

the Great at the beginning of the 4th century BC. Some years later, the Greeks in their turn were ousted by an Indian ruler, Chandragupta Maurya. This was the foundation (about 320 BC) of the Maurya dynasty, the first great Indian dynasty. Gradually, the Maurya extended their domination over all India, with the exception of the south. The most famous of their rulers was Asoka, who came to the throne around 269 BC. He converted to Buddhism, a religion founded in India in the 5th century BC, and encouraged its expansion. He left his mark on the country by building roads, wells and hospitals. We have much more information about his reign than that of other emperors, because Asoka had the text of his decrees (or edicts) engraved on rocks and on great pillars of stone that have been found in all parts of India.

Warrior kingdoms

After Asoka's death in 232 BC, his successors could not prevent the division of the empire. The Maurya dynasty was overthrown about 185 BC. India was then split into various small kingdoms, a division that lasted nearly five centuries. The north of the country was invaded several times, first by the Scythians and then by the Kushan nomads from Central Asia. Then, in the 4th century AD, a new king from the north of India, Chandragupta I, founded the Gupta dynasty. This dynasty unified India until the Huns, a people from Central Asia, invaded in the following century. □

Drum from Dong Son ▲

This bronze drum was found at Dong Son (modern Vietnam), in the tomb of a tribal chief who lived between the 6th and the 3rd centuries BC. It was almost certainly used for religious ceremonies, perhaps to bring the rain that is so vital for rice growing. This was the period of the Hung dynasty, which ruled Vietnam until it was conquered by China in 111 BC.

The stupa of Sanchi, a Buddhist religious building of the 2nd century BC. ▶

BC

6000 First Chinese civilizations.
c. 2000 First Chinese dynasty, the Xia, according to legend founded by Yu the Great with the help of a dragon that emerged from the Yellow River.
c. 1800-1025 Period of the Shang kings.
c. 1500 Invention of Chinese writing, made up of ideograms.
1025 Overthrow of the Shang dynasty and seizure of power by the Zhou.
551-479 Life of Confucius.
481-221 Period of the Warring States: China is split into several military states.
225 Building of the first fortifications that later, in the reign of Qin Shi Huangdi, formed part of the Great Wall of China.
221 Qin Shi Huangdi unifies the kingdom and becomes the first emperor of China.
206 Beginning of the reign of the imperial Han dynasty.

AD

220 End of Han rule.
220-581 Division of the empire into several kingdoms. Expansion of Buddhism in China.

In China, as in Mesopotamia, Egypt and India, people first settled along the great rivers. From 2000 BC, major kingdoms emerged during the gradual unification of the country.

China

The first Chinese civilizations developed around 6000 BC on the banks of the Chang Jiang (Yangtze), the Long River, and of the Huang He, the Yellow River. Around 2000 BC, the Chinese of these fertile regions lived in villages, grew rice, wheat and millet and raised pigs. Here, in the north and center of the lands that form modern China, the country's first kingdoms emerged.

A very ancient civilization

According to legend, the first Chinese dynasty, the Xia, was founded around 2000 BC by Yu the Great, aided by a dragon that emerged from the Yellow River. For historians, the history of China begins some two centuries later, with the Shang dynasty that ruled China for a great part of the 2nd millennium. The Chinese thought that China, which they called the Middle Kingdom, was at the center of the world. Their ruler was considered the Son of Heaven. Very little is known about this period. We do know, however, that the Chinese worked bronze, that they perfected a shiny, smooth, resin-based coating (lacquer) and that they invented, around 1500 BC, a script in which the characters (or ideograms) represent ideas.

Military states

The Shang dynasty struggled against attacks by the nomadic peoples of neighboring regions. Weakened, it was overthrown about 1025 BC and a new dynasty—the Zhou—took power. For several centuries, the Zhou managed to maintain unity. They perfected their weapons: iron swords, crossbows, war chariots and siege engines. They also built fortifications along the northern frontier to defend themselves from invasions by neighboring peoples. From 481 BC, Zhou China split into several military states that waged almost constant war for the next 300 years. During this period of the Warring States, followers of the sage Confucius traveled the country, preaching moderation to the kings. They wished to see peace. For Confucius, the ruler's role was to maintain harmony between his subjects and to be an example through his good conduct and through the respect that he accorded to his ancestors and to the gods. The principles of Confucius, which instill obedience to the ruler, deeply influenced Chinese society.

Bronze vase ▲ from the Shang period.

Qin, the first emperor

The richest and most powerful of the Warring States was that of the Qin, in the northwest of China. In 221 BC, its ruler, Qin Shi Huangdi, unified China by imposing his rule over the other states to become the

The Great Wall of China, built in the 3rd century BC.

first emperor of China. To reinforce the unity of the country, Qin Shi Huangdi imposed the same coinage for all and the same laws. He had a system of wide roads built to link his capital, Xian, with the most remote regions of his territory. He also had canals dug to promote trade. To protect his empire, he had the fortifications built by his predecessors linked and extended east and west, constructing a very long wall, the Great Wall of China. Qin Shi Huangdi died in 210 BC. As the Son of Heaven, he was buried in a sumptuous tomb along with thousands of terra-cotta warrior figures to defend him in the afterworld. Four years after his death, a new dynasty took power, the Han. The Han held onto power for more than 400 years and extended the empire's territory still farther. After the Han came a period of further unrest. By this time, the Chinese had learned how to manufacture paper. There was an expansion of literature and arts, and after the arrival of Buddhism from India, Buddhist art flourished. The sciences, in particular medicine and mathematics, made enormous advances. Trade links grew between the Chinese Empire and the Roman world. The Romans paid in gold coins for silk woven and dyed in China. The routes taken by the trade caravans formed the Silk Road. □

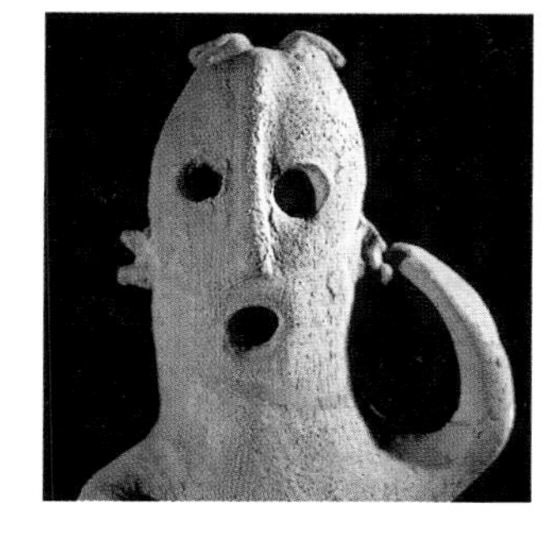

Japanese statuette ▲

This earthenware Japanese warrior is a *haniwa* and was found in an immense tomb known as a *kofun*. It dates from the 4th century AD. In Japan, the Neolithic period lasted until the foundation of the first Japanese state, the Yamato empire, in the 1st century AD. Archeologists think that the Japanese at first sacrificed servants and animals, which they placed in the tombs of important people, and that later these human sacrifices were substituted for by terra-cotta cylinders surmounted by figurines like this one. In the Emperor Nintoku's tomb, near Osaka, there were more than 20,000 such figures to accompany the dead ruler. The Yamato empire, which was influenced by Korea, gave way to another empire in the 6th century AD.

Chariot of the Warring States period (5th century BC). ▼

The army of Qin

The Chinese emperor Qin Shi Huangdi died in 210 BC and was buried near Xian, his capital, with more than 7,000 terra-cotta soldiers. It was a tradition that Chinese leaders were buried with their soldiers and servants, killed to follow their master in death. Pictured here are model infantrymen (foot soldiers) of the imperial army in combat position. They measure 1.80 m (6 ft), slightly taller than the average height of the Chinese at that time. In the following centuries, the Han emperors also had themselves buried with terra-cotta figures, but these were smaller (above, a Han archer).

The Greek civilization that emerged around 2000 BC dominated the Mediterranean basin and Asia Minor until the 1st century BC. It became a political, cultural and artistic model that later influenced the Romans.

Greece

BC

2000-1450 Flourishing of the Cretan civilization.

1800 Arrival of the Achaeans in Greece.

1600-1200 Kingdom of Mycenae.

1200-900 Period known as the dark ages.

c. 850 Emergence of the first Greek city-states.

490-479 Persian wars between the Persians and the Greeks.

443-429 Pericles, *strategos* of Athens.

431-404 Peloponnesian War. Victory of Sparta; end of Athenian supremacy over the Greek city-states.

338 King Philip II of Macedonia conquers the Greek city-states.

336 Alexander succeeds his father Philip, becoming king of Macedonia.

323 Death of Alexander the Great. His empire is divided into several kingdoms.

146-30 The Hellenistic kingdoms become Roman provinces. End of the Hellenistic period.

The large peninsula and numerous islands of Greece were split in ancient times into many small independent city-states, formed of a city and its surrounding countryside. The most important were Athens and Sparta. After several centuries of prosperity, these city-states were conquered in the 4th century BC by the king of Macedonia, Alexander (who became known as "the Great"). In the 2nd century BC, Greece became a Roman province.

Priest-king ▶ of Knossos in Crete.

The epoch of the palaces

The first Greek civilization developed on the island of Crete in the Aegean Sea from 2000 to 1450 BC. There, the remains of the city of Knossos (the capital of the legendary king Minos) and of an immense palace have been discovered, bearing witness to a rich civilization. From 1800 BC, the Achaeans, who originated in central Europe, populated the Greek mainland and islands. Among the kingdoms they founded, one of the most important was Mycenae in the Peloponnese (the central region of Greece). Achaean life was organized around their palaces, which were fortified buildings with enormous walls. Gold objects found in their tombs are witness to the power and richness of Mycenae. Little is known about Greek history from 1200 to 900 BC. The Achaean kingdoms disappeared and a people from the north, the Dorians, settled in the Peloponnese. This period, called the dark ages, is described in two poems from about the 8th century BC, *The Iliad* and *The Odyssey*, attributed to Homer. These long epic poems mix legend and real events, recounting episodes of the war waged by the Achaeans against Troy, a city in Asia Minor.

The city-states

In the 9th century BC, the kingdoms gave way to the first city-states. Each of these had its own laws, and two states, Athens and Sparta, competed to dominate all Greece. From the 6th century BC, the citizens of Athens took part in the government of the state. This is what is known as democracy (from the Greek *demos*, people, and *kratos*,

The Parthenon on the Acropolis of Athens dates from the 5th century BC.

power). Not all the people who lived in Athens were citizens, however: foreigners, women and slaves had no political rights. Athenian democracy was organized around an assembly, a council of 500 citizens and a law court. The assembly, made up of all the citizens, voted on the laws drawn up by the council and decided to make peace or wage war. Nine archons, chief magistrates drawn by lot, enforced the decisions of the assembly. Justice was dispensed by a jury of citizens drawn by lot. Ten elected generals (*strategos* in Greek) commanded the army. Sparta, the city-state that rivaled Athens, was governed by two kings and a council of 28 elder-senators, the *gerons*. It was an oligarchy (from the Greek *oligos*, few, and *archein*, to command), a political system in which power was held by a minority of the citizens. The inhabitants of Sparta were soldiers in the service of the state, which strictly controlled their lives. After a harsh education, the life of the Spartans was dedicated to military training and war.

The Persian wars

Around 500 BC, the Persians came through Asia Minor and attacked the Greek city-states. So began the Persian wars, which lasted until the middle of the 5th century BC. Under Athenian command, the Greeks won a victory at Marathon in 490 BC and at Salamis in 480 BC. Taking advantage of these successes, Athens brought all the Greek city-states under its authority and formed the Delian League. Using the league, it formed what was in fact an empire. The 5th century BC was the era of Athens' splendor. The sculptor Phidias (c. 490-431 BC) directed the building of the Parthenon on the hill called the Acropolis that was the center of the civil, religious and political life of the city. Athens was at this time an important cultural center and meeting place for artists, writers and philosophers, such as Sophocles (496-406 BC), Euripides (480-406 BC) and Socrates (470-399 BC). □

The Trojan war ▲

The legendary Trojan war is the theme of *The Iliad*, a poem written down in the 8th century BC. The poem tells the story of the Greek heroes during their war against the city of Troy in Asia Minor. Agamemnon, king of Mycenae, led the expedition to recapture his brother's wife, Helen, who had been carried off by Paris, son of the king of Troy. Among the Greek warriors were Achilles and Ajax, pictured here playing dice. Troy was captured after a ten-year siege when the Greek hero, Odysseus, tricked the Trojans into bringing inside their walls an immense wooden horse in which soldiers were hiding. This story is not without some foundation: excavations have revealed that very rich cities existed at the sites of both Troy and Mycenae.

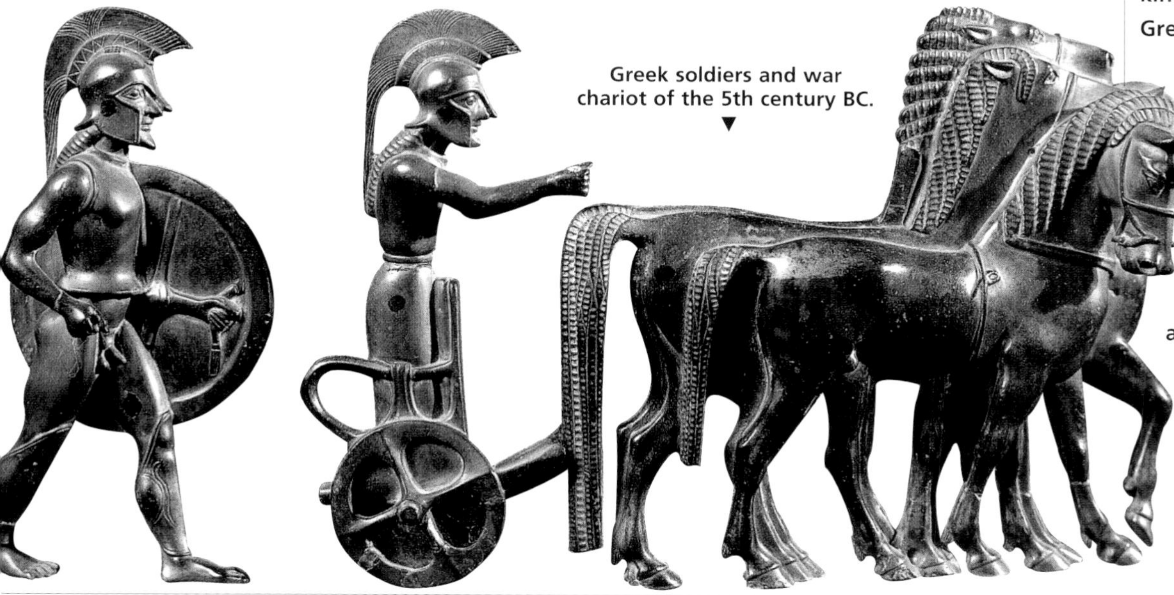

Greek soldiers and war chariot of the 5th century BC. ▼

Alexander the Great, king of Macedonia, at the battle of Issus.

The end of the city-states and the empire of

The philosopher Plato ▲ and his disciples

The word *philosophy* means in Greek "love of wisdom." The Greek philosophers gave profound thought to define what is good, beautiful and true. Plato (427-348 BC), seen here surrounded by his pupils, passed on through his writings the ideas of one of the greatest Greek philosophers, Socrates (470-399 BC). Socrates himself never wrote a book. Plato, who had been one of his main pupils, made him the central character of his dialogues. Plato shows Socrates as someone who taught people to discover for themselves the truth about the world. He also tells of the death of Socrates. Condemned to die by the city of Athens, the philosopher had to take hemlock, a poison.

The dominance of Athens over the other city-states caused conflicts throughout all Greece. Taking advantage of the interstate rivalry, King Philip II of Macedonia set out in the 4th century BC to conquer Greece. His task was completed by his son, Alexander the Great, who extended the empire far to the east.

The city-states at war

Athens took considerable profit from the Delian League, which it controlled. This stirred up jealousy in other city-states and set off the Peloponnesian War. From 431 to 404 BC, Athens fought Sparta, each in alliance with other city-states. When the Athenians were finally defeated, they had to give up their empire. King Philip II (382-336 BC) of Macedonia in the north of Greece took advantage of these rivalries and with his powerful army defeated the Greeks at the battle of Chaeronea in 338 BC. He then brought all the Greek city-states together in the Corinthian League, of which he was military commander, and so ended their independence.

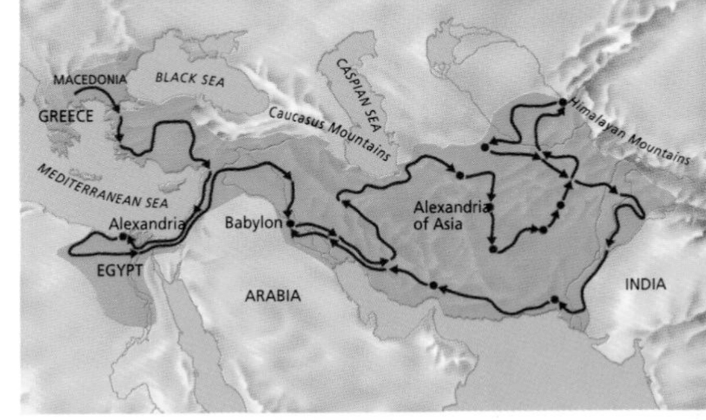

▲ The conquests of Alexander

In less than fifteen years, Alexander crossed Asia and went beyond the limits of the known world. Along the way, he founded cities, almost all of which he named Alexandria. He died suddenly, before having time to realize his next project—rounding the Arabian Peninsula by ship.

Spartan soldier in battle. ▼

The Persian king Darius III at the battle of Issus.

Alexander

Alexander the Great

When Philip died in 336 BC, he was succeeded by his twenty-year-old son, Alexander. Step by step, Alexander was to form one of the greatest empires of the ancient world. First he fought the Persians in Asia Minor, defeating their king, Darius III, at the battle of Issus in 333 BC. Then he occupied Phoenicia (present-day Lebanon) and Egypt, where he founded the city of Alexandria. He continued east and vanquished the army of Darius III in 331 BC at Arbela, in Mesopotamia. Alexander then became ruler of Persia. From 330 to 327 BC he continued to advance, in spite of the weariness of his army, across Asia through what is now Afghanistan and reached the banks of the Indus in what is now Pakistan. In 323 BC he died at Babylon, in Mesopotamia. Alexander the Great was not only a conqueror. Scholars and geographers accompanied him on his campaigns. He was curious about the civilizations that he encountered and tried to blend Greek and Eastern cultures, forming the Hellenistic civilization (from *Hellenes*, the name that the Greeks called themselves).

Hellenistic civilization

On his death, Alexander the Great left an immense and still unorganized empire with no clear succession. After fifty years of struggle, his generals split up the empire: Antigonus took Macedonia (creating the Antigonid dynasty), Seleucus took Asia Minor (Seleucid dynasty) and Ptolemy ruled Egypt (the Ptolemaic dynasty). In these Hellenistic kingdoms, the sovereigns were all-powerful and looked upon as gods. Eastern practices and cults mixed with Greek culture.

The official language was Greek. The Hellenistic period ended with the Roman conquest of the Hellenistic kingdoms between the 2nd and 1st century BC. The arts, beliefs and customs of this civilization were to persist in the Roman Empire.

Alexandria of Egypt

Founded in 332 BC by Alexander the Great, the city of Alexandria at the mouth of the Nile became the capital of the Ptolemy kings of Egypt. From the 2nd century BC to the Roman conquest of Egypt in 30 BC, Alexandria was the largest city in the Mediterranean world, with around 500,000 inhabitants. It was a melting pot of different peoples. The lighthouse in its harbor (later destroyed) was one of the Seven Wonders of the ancient world. The Egyptian kings were patrons of the arts and advanced the sciences. They set up the Museum, where poets, philosophers and mathematicians lived, worked and taught. Alexandria was also famous for its library, the most prestigious in the ancient world. □

◂ Bronze horse and child, 2nd century BC

This bronze sculpture is an example of Greek art from the Hellenistic period.

The Persians

After 700 BC, the Persians were settled in present-day Iran. They were conquerors who threw off the control of the Medes to seize the countries around them, creating a vast empire that included Asia Minor, Mesopotamia and Egypt. This empire was divided into provinces under governors known as satraps. ▾

In the 8th century BC, Rome was only a small town on the banks of the Tiber River in Italy. This settlement gave its name to one of the greatest states of the ancient world and one of the first enduring empires.

Rome

The city of Rome was founded around 753 BC. The last Roman emperor was deposed in AD 476. Over these 1200 years, Rome was first a town ruled by a king, later a republic and finally the capital of an empire that controlled the Mediterranean world from Europe to Asia.

Early Rome

According to legend, Rome was founded in 753 BC by the twins Romulus and Remus. The two boys had been abandoned as babies and found by a she-wolf that suckled them, saving their lives. When they grew up, they founded a town beside the Tiber to which Romulus, after killing his brother, gave his name—Rome. In memory of this legend, the she-wolf became the symbol of the city. Archeology has shown that Rome had emerged by the 8th century BC from the union of a number of villages sited on seven hills along the Tiber. The people of these villages were Sabines and Latins, who were then masters of central Italy. In the next century, Rome was conquered by a neighboring people, the Etruscans. The city, which was then ruled by a king, grew and developed its form of government. In 509 BC, the people of Rome ousted the Etruscans and set up a republic.

The Roman Republic

Under the Republic, the citizens of Rome met in assemblies called *comitiae* and each year elected their representatives, the magistrates. From the latter, two consuls were chosen: they controlled political life and commanded the armies. At the head of the state was the senate. This body was made up of senior magistrates and oversaw all the important proceedings of the Republic. At first, only the *patricians*, landowning members of aristocratic Roman families, could elect magistrates and take part in the city's politics. In the 3rd century BC, farmers, traders and artisans—the *plebeians* (in Latin *plebs* means "people")—also won the right to vote. Slaves and foreigners were excluded from political life, as were women, who had to look after the household.

The first conquests

From the beginnings of the Republic, Rome extended its territory in Italy. Its military success was due to a large and well-organized army formed of citizens called up in time of war and marshaled in legions. The Romans were very patriotic and accepted strict

◄ **The she-wolf suckling Romulus and Remus is the symbol of Rome.**

BC

753 Founding of Rome.
509-27 Roman republic.
287 Plebeians gain equality with the patricians.
264-146 Punic Wars between Rome and Carthage.
107-48 Rivalry of generals in Rome; civil war.
44 Caesar becomes consul and then dictator for life. He is assassinated by Brutus and others.
27 Beginning of the Roman Empire. Octavian becomes emperor, taking the name Augustus.

AD

54-68 Reign of Nero.
79-81 Reign of Titus.
98-117 Reign of Trajan.
161-180 Reign of Marcus Aurelius.
211-217 Reign of Caracalla.
306-337 Reign of Constantine.
330 Constantinople is capital of the Empire.
395 Division of the Empire into the Eastern Roman Empire and the Western Roman Empire.
476 End of the Western Roman Empire.

Samnite warriors of the 4th century BC, conquered by the Romans.

discipline to defend their country. By the 3rd century BC, they dominated all of present-day Italy and set off to conquer the Mediterranean basin. Rome then came into conflict with Carthage, a powerful city in North Africa. The two cities fought three long wars, the Punic Wars, over more than a hundred years. One of the most famous episodes of this struggle began in 218 BC. Leaving Africa with an army that included elephants, the Carthaginian general Hannibal marched across Spain and over the Alps to attack the Romans from the north. He won a number of great victories before finally being defeated. The wars ended in 146 BC with Rome as the victor. Carthage was destroyed, and its territory became the Roman province of Africa.

A patrician, carrying sculpted heads of his ancestors. ►

The end of the Republic

After the fall of Carthage, Rome continued its conquests. From the 2nd to the 1st century BC, it took control of Spain, Gaul and a number of the Hellenistic kingdoms (Macedonia, Greece and later the kingdom of Pontus, in present-day Turkey) governed by the successors of Alexander the Great. Masters of the Mediterranean basin, from this period the Romans called the Mediterranean "our sea." Their conquests brought to Rome enormous quantities of gold, wheat and slaves, which radically transformed society. The gap between rich and poor widened, while respect for tradition was weakened by contact with new cultures. Exploiting the popularity of their conquests, Roman generals sought to seize power. Civil wars broke out, menacing the existence of the Republic. Cicero, a politician and orator, tried to defend it but was assassinated in 43 BC. Julius Caesar, famous as the conqueror of Gaul and victorious over the other generals, made himself head of state in 48 BC. The senate granted him full powers: sole consul, head of the army and religious chief. Caesar succeeded in having himself elected dictator for life. In 44 BC, he was assassinated by republicans led by one of his friends, Brutus. □

Carthage

This glass amulet was discovered at Carthage, a city founded by the Phoenicians around 800 BC on the coast of present-day Tunisia. The Phoenicians were skillful sailors and enterprising merchants, operating from the ports of what is now Lebanon. Around 1200 BC, they invented an alphabetic script with 22 letters, the forerunner of the Greek and Latin alphabets.

The city of Carthage was governed by its richest merchants, who dominated the Mediterranean with their war fleet and an army of paid mercenaries. The Carthaginians were masters of the western Mediterranean from the 6th century BC. The first clash with Rome came in the 3rd century BC. The city of Carthage was captured and destroyed by the Romans in 146 BC.

Scene of a ball game from a 1st-century wall painting.

The Roman Empire

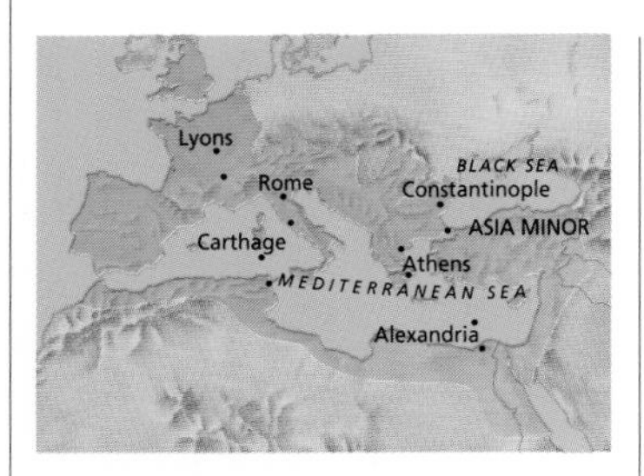

The Roman Empire ▲
The Empire reached its maximum extent in the 2nd century AD.

A barbarian horseman
In the first centuries AD, the number of barbarians on the frontiers of the Roman Empire increased. Many served in the Roman army. ▼

In the 3rd century, upheavals in Central Asia forced nomads to find new lands to the west. These nomads ousted the Vandals, Goths, Burgundians, Angles and Saxons, who then invaded the Roman Empire. In the middle of the 5th century, the Huns, originally from Asia, burst into Gaul. Their leader, Attila, threatened Rome and founded an empire that broke up after his death.

After Caesar's assassination, a new struggle for power broke out among the Roman generals. Octavian, one of Caesar's adopted sons, won the battle of Actium in 30 BC against Cleopatra, queen of Egypt. He then occupied Egypt, which became a Roman province. This conquest confirmed Octavian's power. He ended the Republic and founded the Roman Empire.

The emperor

In 27 BC, Octavian became the first Roman emperor, taking the name Augustus, which means "venerated." The senate still existed, but the emperor in effect held all power. He appointed its representatives and made the laws; he was head of the armies (*imperator*, in Latin), and *pontifex maximus* or religious chief. A cult—the imperial cult—was dedicated to him. On his death, he was deified and temples were built for him. From 27 BC to AD 235 four dynasties succeeded each other at the head of the empire: the Julio-Claudians (including Nero), the Flavians (including Titus), the Antonines (including Trajan and Marcus Aurelius) and the Severians (including Caracalla).

The Pax Romana

During the first two centuries of the Empire, Rome experienced a period of peace and exceptional prosperity, taking advantage of its immense territories, which now stretched from Europe to Asia. All the conquered territories became Roman provinces, administered by the emperor's representatives, the governors. Products from the provinces were brought to Rome by sea or by an impressive road network. The peoples of the provinces adopted the way of life and laws of the Romans. Rome's architecture served as a model for the new cities that were built. In AD 212, all free men of the Empire were granted Roman citizenship: they then had the same rights as the Romans, being able to vote and take part in the politics of Rome. A system of fortifications, the *limites*, was built over a distance of more than 9,000 km (5,600 miles) to mark the boundaries of the empire and to protect its frontiers from foreign peoples, whom the Romans called "barbarians." Barbarian soldiers were also recruited to help in the defense of each *limes*.

Gladiators fighting in the circus. ▲

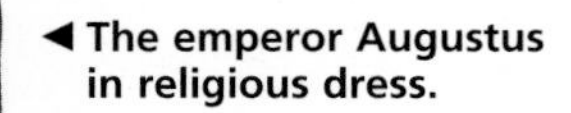

◄ The emperor Augustus in religious dress.

Theatrical performance as shown on a mosaic of 70 BC found at Pompeii.

The fall of the empire

From the 3rd century AD, Germanic peoples from the east—including Goths, Vandals and Burgundians—fled before the Huns, another people from Central Asia, and sought new lands to settle. Neither the Roman army nor the *limites* could stop them. For protection, towns were walled, and in AD 275 the emperor Aurelian had a rampart, the Aurelian wall, built in Rome. In AD 406, huge numbers of barbarians crossed the Rhine in invasions that paralyzed trade between the provinces and Rome. A new religion, Christianity, began to change the beliefs of the Romans in the 1st century AD. Originating in the Roman province of Palestine, Christianity spread throughout the whole empire. Christians were persecuted, in particular because they refused to join in the imperial cult. Nevertheless, many Roman citizens adopted the new religion, and in AD 313, the emperor Constantine recognized Christianity, which became the official religion of the empire. In time, the empire became impossible to govern and was divided in 395 between the Western Empire with Rome as its capital, and the Eastern Empire with its capital at Constantinople, formerly Byzantium and now Istanbul. In 476, a barbarian general forced the last emperor of the West to abdicate: from then on the Roman empire endured only in Constantinople. □

The Colosseum in Rome

In their amphitheaters or arenas, the Romans organized animal and gladiatorial combats. They also flocked to the circuses to watch chariot races. To keep their popularity, the emperors offered expensive and bloody spectacles. Like Rome, each city of the empire had its arenas, its forum (public meeting place), its thermae (public baths) and in some cases, its circus. In the countryside, the Romans built huge aqueducts to supply towns with water. The whole empire was crossed by solidly built roads, remnants of which can still be found today.

the

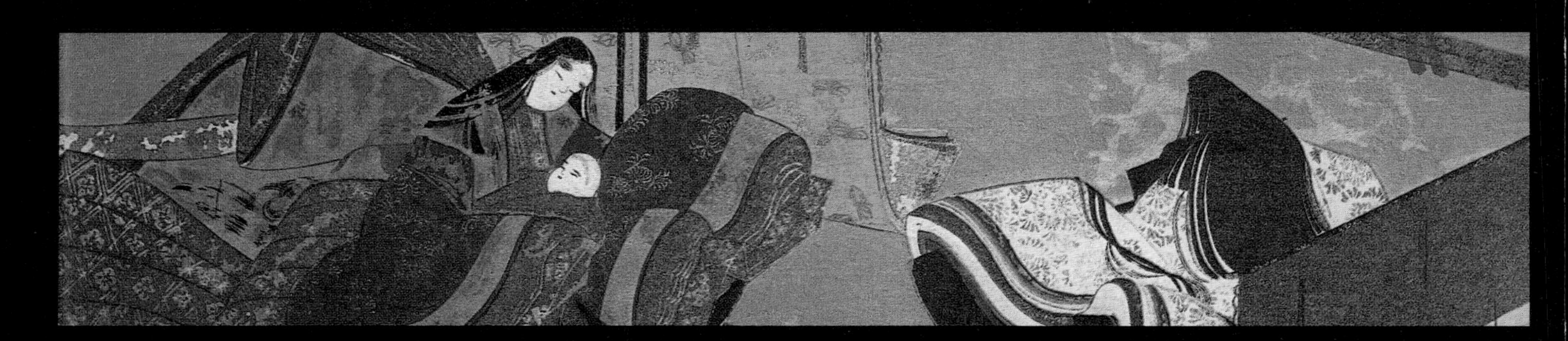

middle ages

The Byzantine Empire, or Eastern Roman Empire, lasted in the countries of the eastern Mediterranean from 395 to 1453. Its capital of Constantinople was a great cultural, religious and political center.

The Byzantine Empire

395 Division of the Roman Empire.
527-565 Reign of Justinian.
6th-7th c. The Slavs invade the Empire. The Arabs conquer Syria and Egypt, provinces of the Empire.
8th c. Crisis of the icons: adoration of religious images is condemned.
1054 Separation of the Church of Rome and the Church of Constantinople.
11th c. The Normans take Sicily and Southern Italy, parts of the Empire. The Turks occupy Asia Minor.
1204 The Fourth Crusade takes Constantinople.
1261 Reconquest of Constantinople by the Byzantine emperor, Michael VIII.
1453 The Turks take Constantinople. End of the Byzantine Empire.

In 395, the Roman Empire was divided in two: the Western Empire, which collapsed in 476 following barbarian invasions, and the Eastern Empire, which became known as the Byzantine Empire. This empire extended all around the Mediterranean, from Greece to Asia Minor and to Northern Africa. Its capital was Constantinople, founded in 330 on the site of the Greek city of Byzantium.

▲ The patriarch Nikephoros blessing the emperor Michael I in 811.

The emperor and the Byzantine church

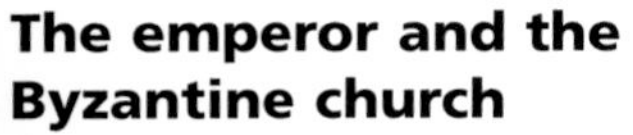

From the 4th century, Christianity was the religion of the Roman Empire. The Byzantine emperor, as master of what remained of this empire, was above all the master of the Christian world. He claimed that his powers came from God, who had chosen him. His subjects prostrated themselves before him and everything concerning him was sacred. On the mosaics adorning the walls of the churches and in the miniatures painted on manuscripts, artists showed him with his head surrounded by a halo of light, like a divine being. One of the most remarkable reigns of the Byzantine era was that of the emperor Justinian. Justinian was a conqueror, who reestablished imperial authority over the western part of the former Roman Empire. He also concerned himself with justice, instructing that all the laws and regulations of the Empire be collated in a single volume, which was named the Code of Justinian. This compilation was written in Greek, the language spoken all over the Byzantine Empire. Justinian had the church of San Vitale built in Ravenna, Italy, and the basilica of St. Sophia in Constantinople. The powers of the emperor were sometimes challenged by the patriarch of Constantinople, head of the Byzantine church and the second most important person in the empire. In the 8th century, the iconoclastic controversy brought numerous believers into conflict with the emperor who believed that Christians attached too much importance to icons, the religious images of saints, and wanted them destroyed. The emperor and his partisans were known as iconoclasts, or "breakers of images." In 1054, another religious conflict between the patriarch of Constantinople and the pope, head of the Roman church, caused the two churches to separate.

◀ The emperor Justinian, from a Byzantine mosaic in the 6th-century church of San Vitale, Ravenna, Italy.

The most beautiful city in the world

Constantinople was built on the Bosporus strait that separates Europe from Asia. Here crossed the gold, silk and spice routes from Asia and Africa, and the amber and fur routes from northern Europe. Constantinople was also an important port, from which merchants and ships from Venice set out for the east. The Byzantine currency, the gold solidus, favored this trade, because the Chinese and Indian merchants preferred it to their own coinage. Around 1000, there were nearly 1 million people living in the rich city

The empress Theodora, wife of Justinian, from the church of San Vitale in Ravenna.

of Constantinople. Like the Romans, the Byzantines had forums as meeting places. At the center of the city was the imperial palace, linked to the hippodrome, where the sport of chariot racing—inherited from Rome—took place.

A threatened empire

From the 6th century, the Byzantine Empire had to repel several waves of invaders. Parts of its territory came under foreign rule. In the north, the Bulgars and the Slavs attacked it along the Danube. In the east, the Muslim Arabs seized Syria and Egypt, the richest provinces of the empire. Still greater dangers arose in the 11th century, when the Seljuk Turks overran Asia Minor and the Normans took Sicily and southern Italy, regions belonging to the empire. In 1204, Constantinople was sacked during the Fourth Crusade, an expedition of Christian knights that set out from western Europe to conquer Jerusalem. The city was reconquered in 1261 by the Byzantine emperor Michael VIII. Attacks by the Serbs and the Ottoman Turks weakened the empire still further, and by the 14th century it was reduced to the city of Constantinople. In 1453, Constantinople was captured by troops of the Ottoman sultan, Mehmed II. The remnant of the Byzantine empire had fallen into the hands of the Turks, who called the city Istanbul. □

Stephen Uros Milutin, king of Serbia ▲

This 13th-century king had himself depicted holding a church to show his generosity toward the Christian church. The Serbs were converted to Christianity in the 10th century. Two Byzantine monks, Cyril and Methodius, brought the religion to the Slavs. The Russian church was founded in 986 by Vladimir, prince of Kiev. After 1453, the Russian capital of Moscow became the center of the Eastern Church.

The city of Constantinople besieged by the Turks in 1453. ▼

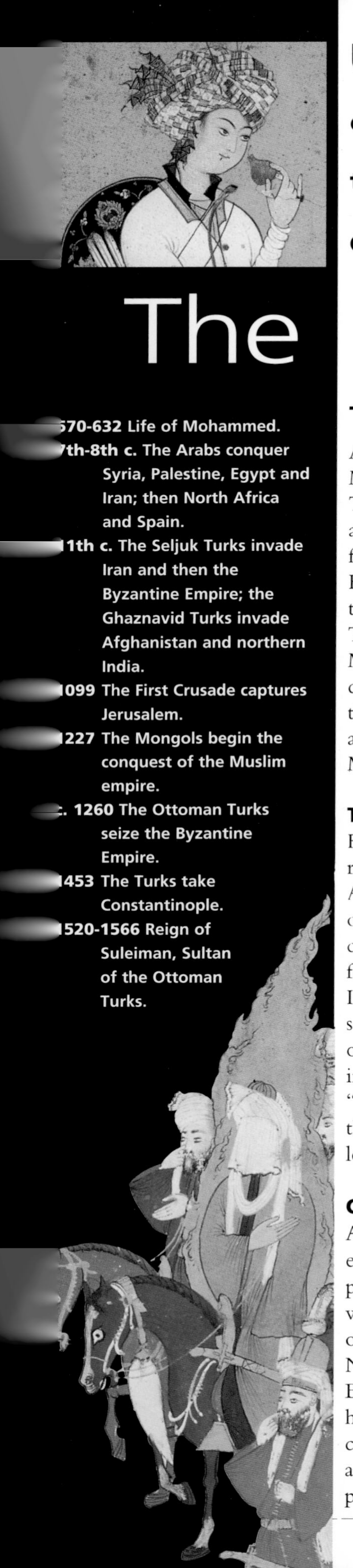

United by their religion of Islam, the Muslims in the 7th century founded an empire that stretched from the Indus to the Mediterranean. Arab scientists made important discoveries and technological advances.

The Muslim world

570-632 Life of Mohammed.
7th-8th c. The Arabs conquer Syria, Palestine, Egypt and Iran; then North Africa and Spain.
11th c. The Seljuk Turks invade Iran and then the Byzantine Empire; the Ghaznavid Turks invade Afghanistan and northern India.
1099 The First Crusade captures Jerusalem.
1227 The Mongols begin the conquest of the Muslim empire.
c. 1260 The Ottoman Turks seize the Byzantine Empire.
1453 The Turks take Constantinople.
1520-1566 Reign of Suleiman, Sultan of the Ottoman Turks.

The history of the Muslim world began in Arabia in 622, when the prophet Mohammed founded the religion of Islam. The Arabs then set out to conquer the world and, by 750, dominated an empire extending from the Mediterranean to the Himalayas. From the 9th-10th century, each region of the empire was in practice independent. The Turks, converts to Islam, continued the Muslim conquests from the 11th to the 16th centuries. All Muslims were conscious that they belonged to a single community. They all spoke and read Arabic, the language of Mohammed and of the Koran.

The origins of the Muslim empire

From 630, Islam took over Arabia. Islam is a religion based on belief in a single God, Allah (see *Religions of the World*). The words of Allah as revealed to Mohammed are contained in the Koran, which sets out the fundamental precepts of the Muslim religion. Islamic law, called the *Sharia*, is the basis of society and of the state and regulates aspects of everyday life. On the death of Mohammed in 632, power passed to the caliphs, or "commanders of the believers," who were at the same time religious, military and political leaders.

Conquests and division

After Mohammed's death, the Arabs in 657 embarked on conquests to convert other peoples to their new religion. For them, this was a *jihad* or holy war. In the east, they occupied Syria, Palestine, Egypt and Iran. In North Africa, they converted the nomadic Berbers. They conquered Spain, but were halted at Poitiers in France in 732. Their conquered provinces or states were administered by military governors or princes, the emirs, who themselves answered to the caliph at the head of the empire. However, after Mohammed's death, Islam divided into two branches: the Sunni and the Shia. The majority of believers, the Sunnites, thought that Mohammed's successor should be chosen from an important family from Mecca. A minority, the Shiites, wanted to choose the caliph from the descendants of Ali, Mohammed's son-in-law. In the 8th century, a state was set up around Cordoba in Spain that was independent from the caliph, who had established his capital at Baghdad in Iraq in 750. Many other regions, including Egypt, North Africa and Iran, ceased to obey the caliph of Baghdad in the 9th century.

Entrance to a Muslim college in Morocco.

رسول الله صلى الله عليه به وفي التاسع عشر عرفاة ابي طالب وفي الثاني والعشرين زعمو التقم

ذو القعدة يونس الحوت

في الخامس نزول الكعبة والرحمة من السماء على آدم وفيه رفع ابرهيم واسمعيل القواعد

Extract from an Arab manuscript.

From the 11th century, most of the divided Muslim states gradually came under the rule of the Turks from Central Asia.

Trade and sciences

Muslim civilization was established in the great cities of Iran and Egypt. The conquests enabled Arab merchants to extend their trading activities. Artisans in the cities worked leather, metal, cloth, precious stones and ivory, and finished articles were transported overland by camel caravans. For commercial activities, the Arabs used letters of exchange, or *sakk*, forerunners of checks. Arab civilization was also distinguished by scientific advances, by important discoveries and by technical inventions in the fields of astronomy, navigation and medicine that were later adopted by many other peoples.

Astronomers studied the heavens and the position of the planets. The scientist Al-Biruni (973–1050) demonstrated that the Earth is round. The Arabs perfected the compass, the rudder and the sextant. Mathematics also advanced with the use of zero and the practice of algebra (from the Arab word *al-jabr*, which means "reduction"). Arabic numerals were passed on to Europeans by Muslims, who had learned about them in India. Physicians such as Avicenna (980–1037) studied anatomy, carried out operations with anesthetics and manufactured syrups and medicines from plants. □

◄ Caravan of Arab merchants.

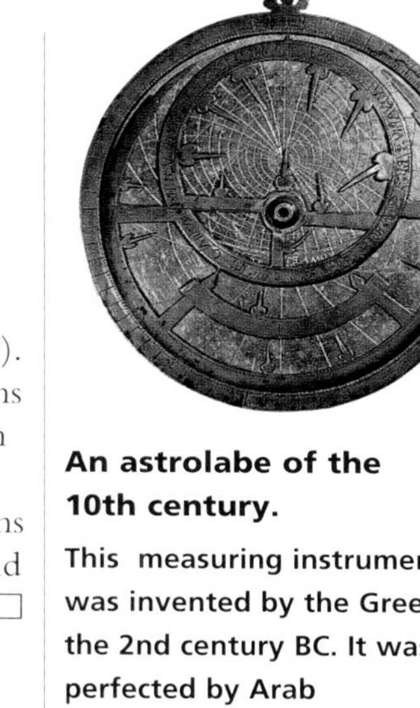

An astrolabe of the 10th century. ▲

This measuring instrument was invented by the Greeks in the 2nd century BC. It was perfected by Arab astronomers who wanted to determine precisely the time of sunrise or sunset, so that the hours for prayer could be set. The astrolabe is made from plates of copper. The largest has an edge graduated in degrees. Moving interior plates correspond to the positions of heavenly bodies at given latitudes.

The Muslim world in the 8th century

Because of the Arab conquests begun in the 7th century, the Muslim world stretched from Arabia to Spain. ▼

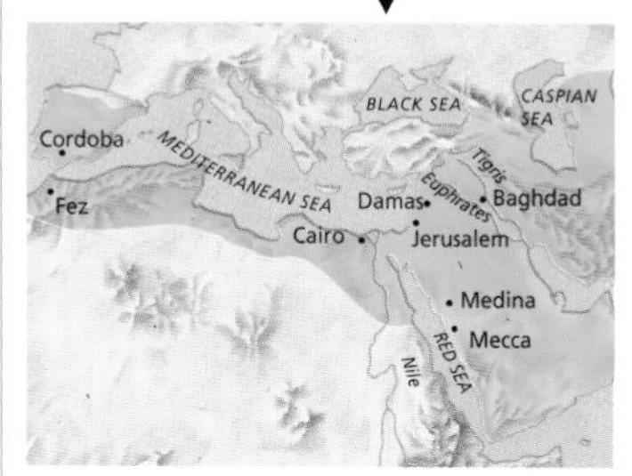

A Mongol camp in 14th-century Iran.

Turks and Mongols

An Arab ship, from a 13th-century manuscript

This boat is crossing the Persian Gulf in the Indian Ocean. Arab merchants look through the portholes, while the ship is manned by dark-skinned sailors, typical of this region where crews are formed of sailors from eastern Africa, Arabia and India.

Islam in Asia

Islam arrived in northern India in the 8th century, spreading

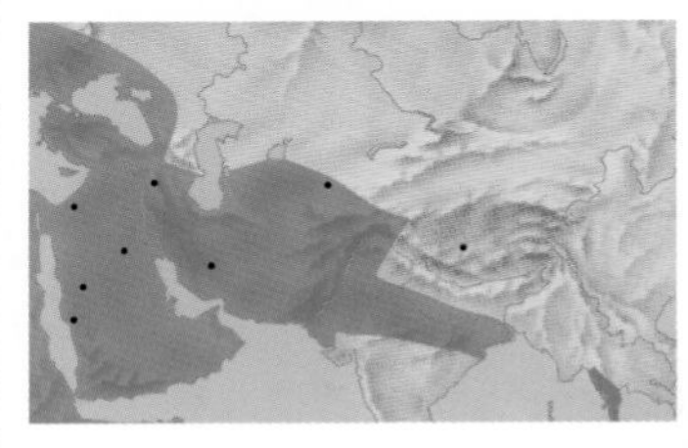

with Arab merchants along the caravan routes and through the ports of the Indian Ocean. From the 12th to the 15th centuries, the Muslim sultanate of Delhi extended across India from the Ganges valley to the Deccan plateau.

From the 11th century, the Muslim world was invaded by Turks and Mongols. These nomadic peoples were from neighboring regions in the east and center of Asia, although they had different languages and customs. The Turks (*türk* means "strong") converted to Islam and became masters of the Muslim world after a period of struggle against the Mongols, who spread terror throughout Asia but did not establish a lasting state.

The conquering Turks

In the 6th century, the Seljuk Turks inhabited the steppes of Central Asia. In the 11th century, they invaded Muslim Asia and conquered Iran. Their leader became a Muslim and an ally of the caliph of Baghdad in 1055, receiving the title of "sultan," or lieutenant of the caliph. The Turks then attacked the Byzantine Empire. After winning the battle of Manzikert in 1071, they dominated the greater part of Asia Minor. The lands taken from the Byzantines formed the Sultanate of Rum. The Turks were the only Muslims to conquer territories at this time. In Spain, the Christians had launched the *Reconquista* (reconquest) of their country, pushing the Muslims back to North Africa. The crusades, expeditions of Christian knights to Palestine, were wars to win back from the Muslims for Christianity the holy places linked with the life and teachings of Jesus. The sultan Saladin (1138–1193) led the fight against the crusaders and became a hero of Islam. In the 11th century

A battle between Iranians and Turks, from the *Books of the Kings*, 1546.

Genghis Khan with two Mongol leaders (Iran, 14th century).

another Turkish dynasty, the Ghaznavids, founded a Muslim state in Afghanistan, later extending their rule across northern India from the capital city of Delhi. In the 13th century, the Muslim Turks were threatened by new and fearsome conquerors who fought on horseback, the Mongols.

The Mongol threat

Unlike the Turks, the Mongols remained in their homeland of Mongolia until the end of the 12th century. Around 1160 an extraordinary chief called Temujin was born there. Temujin, who later took the title of Genghis Khan, meaning "universal emperor," succeeded in 1206 in bringing a number of tribes under his command. He launched expeditions into central Asia and seized China. After his death in 1227, the Mongols set out to conquer the Muslim world. They invaded Iran and advanced as far as Iraq, where in 1258 they captured the Muslim capital, Baghdad, and killed the last caliph. The Mongols then established themselves in Iraq and later moved into southern Russia and Anatolia, the realm of the Seljuk Turks. After their conquests, the Mongols split up into several states, the most important of which was that of the Golden Horde, reaching from the Crimea to southern Russia. In the 14th century, the Muslim world was again threatened by a conqueror from central Asia. Setting out from the city of Samarkand, Tamerlane (1336-1405) conquered and ravaged Iran, Iraq, northern India and Syria. But Tamerlane's empire did not endure after his death. His descendants founded Muslim dynasties that reigned in central Asia and Iran in the 15th century.

▲ Armor and helmet of a 15th-century Ottoman Turk.

The triumph of the Ottoman Turks

Another Turkish people, the Ottomans (so called because of their descent from a chief called Othman) began from 1260 to dismember the Byzantine Empire. The Ottomans completed their conquest by taking Constantinople, the capital of the Empire, in 1453. They had a formidable army of janissaries, who were soldiers carried off from their families as children and raised to become ruthless warriors. In the 16th century, the Ottomans were the principal Muslim power. They took over Syria and Egypt and proclaimed themselves protectors of the holy places of Arabia in succession to the caliphs, the commanders of the believers. The sultan Suleiman, called "the Magnificent" by European princes, reigned from 1520 to 1566. He extended Ottoman rule into North Africa (apart from Morocco) and to central Europe. The Muslim world at this time included three great empires: the Ottoman Empire, master of the eastern Mediterranean and part of Europe, the Empire of Iran and the Mogul Empire in northern India. □

The Qutb Minar in Delhi

This minaret (a tower from which the call to prayer goes out to Muslims) at 72 m (236 ft) is the highest in the world. It bears the name of the prince who had it built: Qutb ub-Din Aybak, a former Turkish slave who in the late 12th century conquered northern India where he founded the sultanate of Delhi. Southern India resisted the Muslims with some difficulty, but its people remained attached to their traditional beliefs and continued to build temples for the many Hindu gods. ▼

The period called the Middle Ages in Europe encompasses the thousand years from the end of the Western Roman Empire in 476 to Christopher Columbus's landing in America in 1492.

End of the Roman Empire.
Beginning of the barbarian kingdoms.
7 The Carolingian dynasty reigns over France and Germany.
Charlemagne is crowned emperor of the West.
Wave of barbarian invasions in Europe.
Division of Charlemagne's empire into three kingdoms.
Otto I founds the Holy Roman Empire.
Beginning of the reign of the Capetians in France.
Conquest of England by William the Conqueror at the battle of Hastings.
270 Crusades in the Near East.
453 Hundred Years' War between France and England.
353 Black Death in Europe.
The Spanish take Granada from the Moors: end of the Reconquista.
Discovery of America by Christopher Columbus.
entury Beginning of the Renaissance in Italy.

Europe in the

◀ Visigoth soldier.

Roman civilization in Western Europe seemed to have disappeared under the shock of the barbarian invasions from the 5th to the 10th centuries. But it survived and took hold in northern and eastern Europe when these regions were converted to Christianity. The society of this time was warlike and violent, as central power grew weak and gradually disappeared. Men ensured their safety by binding themselves with oaths of loyalty. The 13th century, a time of building strong castles and impressive cathedrals, saw prosperity but was followed by a period of crises and disasters. It was at this time that the kingdoms began to form that later developed into the modern European states.

The barbarians

During the 5th century, the barbarians settled in what was formerly the Roman Empire. In England, the Angles and Saxons ousted the Celtic populations; the Scots, in the north, gave their name to Scotland. The Vandals moved through western Europe and into North Africa; the Ostrogoths took Italy; Gaul was divided between the Visigoths, the Burgundians and the Franks. The barbarians were organized into tribes and clans led by kings who were tribal chiefs, chosen by their warriors. There were no rules of succession. On the death of a king, his sons divided his kingdom and fought to increase their territory. Their justice, unlike Roman justice, imposed not punishments but damages in money, to restrict personal vengeance.

The authority of the Church

The barbarian kings took the Roman emperors as examples, and they also gradually converted to

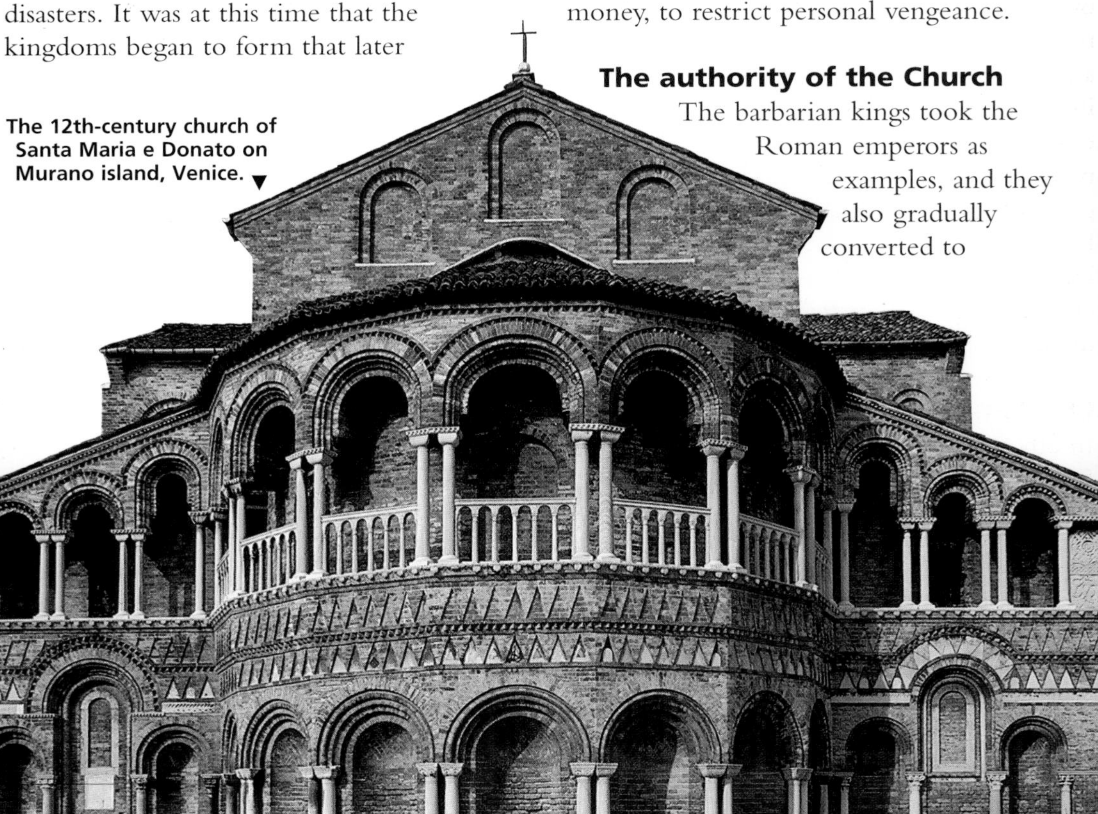

The 12th-century church of Santa Maria e Donato on Murano island, Venice. ▼

William the Conqueror at the battle of Hastings, shown on the 11th-century Bayeux tapestry.

Middle Ages

Coronation of Charlemagne by Pope Leo III in 800. ▼

Christianity, the religion of the Roman Empire. The Christian church was then the only stable authority in the West. It maintained the use of Latin and kept the administrative divisions of the Roman Empire in its dioceses, placing a bishop at the head of each. But pagan practices persisted. Country people continued to believe in fairies and goblins and to hold festivals to ensure good harvests or to cure an illness. The only stone buildings of the period were monasteries, churches and cathedrals. The 10th century marks the beginning of Romanesque art.

Charlemagne, a European emperor

In 8th-century Gaul and Germania (modern France and western Germany), a Frankish family allied to the pope founded the dynasty of the Carolingians, which reigned in Europe from 751 to 987. The name Carolingian comes from the Latin *Carolus*, Charles, as the dynasty traced itself to Charles Martel. His grandson, Charles the Great, or Charlemagne, built an empire. He unified Gaul, took the north of Italy from the Lombards and conquered Germania. He tried to reestablish the authority of the sovereign by appointing inspectors, the *missi dominici*, responsible for overseeing the regions making up the empire. As defender of Christianity, he fought the Muslims of Spain and converted the Germans. In 800, Charlemagne was crowned emperor of the West by the pope. At his capital of Aix-la-Chapelle, the emperor brought together the greatest scholars in Europe. The Carolingian Empire continued under the reign of Louis the Pious (814-840), son and successor of Charlemagne.

Dangers and divisions

Europe suffered a wave of invasions in the 9th century. The East was attacked by the Avars and Magyars, ousted from their territories by the Turks. In the north, Vikings from Scandinavia ravaged the French and English coasts. In 843, by the treaty of Verdun, Charlemagne's empire was divided into three kingdoms. In the west, the kingdom of France was governed from 987 by the Capetians. Germania in the east became, in 962, the Holy Roman Empire under Otto. The central part, which included the east of France and areas of Germania and of Italy, was rapidly absorbed through conquest into the other two kingdoms. In each kingdom, power was held by the great lords, so that William, Duke of Normandy, was more powerful than the king of France. In 1066, by William's victory at the battle of Hastings, he became the Conqueror, master of England, and formed a state that included the duchy of Normandy and the kingdom of England. In the 10th century, the Danes, Swedes, Magyars and Poles of north and central Europe converted and founded Christian kingdoms. □

The Vikings

The Oseberg ship found in Norway (above) was preserved by the clay in which it was buried in the 7th century as a tomb for a Viking princess. Such ships, called drakkars, were built of overlapping planks and were very light. They carried warriors who were capable of rapid maneuvering with their oars and of carrying their ship overland when necessary. A prow figurehead such as the one below inspired terror in people on shore.

A man devoured by a monster, from an 11th–12th century Romanesque church in France.

Feudal society

A crusader ▲

"Crusader" comes from the word *cross*, because the crusaders wore a cloth cross sewn to their clothes when they went to fight in the Holy Land. Following the First Crusade, they founded Christian states there. The later crusades were intended to prevent the Muslims from recapturing these territories.

Dubbing

The young noble is being dubbed a knight. In the religious ceremony of dubbing, he prayed for an entire night and then swore to defend and protect the weak. ▼

Krak-des-Chevaliers, ▶ a fortress of the 12th–13th century built by the crusaders in Syria.

The authority of the state—in effect, the emperor or the king—was weak at the beginning of the Middle Ages. Personal bonds were the cement of society. Each man was bound to other greater or lesser men by oaths of allegiance and by gifts. This system is called feudalism. Feudal society was divided into three groups: the knights, the clergy and the peasants.

Those who fought

In the Middle Ages, war was continuous. It became an activity for "specialists," the knights. These soldiers were the nobility, the highest social category, to which they belonged by hereditary title. From the 12th century, young nobles were dubbed knights during a religious ceremony. Military equipment was perfected: stirrups made it possible to stay in the saddle, and metal armor replaced leather armor. Society in the Middle Ages was organized like a pyramid, with lords and knights bound in homage by an oath of allegiance. At the top of the pyramid was the king, who as supreme sovereign was the most powerful of the lords. Then came the great vassals, lords under allegiance to the king, and finally the ordinary lords. In exchange for his allegiance, the vassal received a fief (*feodus* in Latin: hence the term *feudalism*). Fiefs were usually estates on which castles were built. The feudal system began in the Carolingian Empire and spread over all Europe. Lords exercised the powers of a sovereign: they meted out justice, minted coins and collected taxes. The church tried to moderate the activities of the knights by obliging them to observe "the truce of God," a period during which wars ceased.

Those who prayed

In a profoundly Christian world, the Church played a very important role. It owned vast estates and collected taxes. It founded hospitals for the sick and very poor. The officers of the Church formed the clergy. The secular clergy were priests who lived "in the world" with

◀ An armored knight the 13th century, fr Florence.

Peace and Hope represented on a golden altar, an example of 12th-century Danish Romanesque art.

the faithful. The regular clergy comprised the monks, organized into monastic orders, who followed a strict rule and lived in abbeys, dedicating themselves to prayer, study and work. From the 10th century, the monastic order of the Benedictines, led by the abbey of Cluny, founded numerous abbeys. Other monastic orders, such as the Cistercians, imposed a very austere rule of life. The head of the Christian church, the pope of Rome, controlled his own state. He opposed kings, either in the name of religion or to affirm his authority. The pope also encouraged knights to join crusades, military expeditions against the Muslims, with the goal of regaining control of the holy places in Jerusalem. Eight crusades took place from the 11th to the 13th centuries. Thousands of other believers made pilgrimages to the holy places of the Christian world, such as Rome or Santiago de Compostela in Spain.

Those who worked

In the Middle Ages, 90 percent of the population was made up of peasants who worked for a lord or the church, to whom they paid taxes or rents. These were payable in money or in kind, that is, in grain, wine, livestock or in workdays (corvée). Living conditions were harsh. People depended on harvests that were often poor when the winter was too cold or when war ravaged the countryside. Famines and epidemics were frequent. Many children did not reach adulthood and the population hardly grew at all. Peasants were either free men (called villeins) or serfs, who were attached to the land and had no right to leave it. Serfdom was widespread in the 11th and 12th centuries in France and in England but rarer in northern and eastern Europe. In these sparsely populated regions, lords offered freedom to peasants who settled in new territories. □

The peasants

Dressed in their best clothes, peasants celebrate the return of summer by dancing around a May pole. This scene illustrates the page for the month of May in a book of hours—a 15th-century almanac. Although harsh, the life of the poor was enlivened by many festivals during which work was forbidden. Most of such festivals were Christian. Others dated from ancient times. ▼

The 14th-century town hall of Siena, Italy, from where the city was governed.

The end of the Middle Ages

Battle during the Hundred Years' War

In this picture, the king of England, dressed in red, fights against the king of France, who wears a blue cloak embroidered with fleurs-de-lis. From 1337 to 1453, kings of France and England fought over the throne of France. The English won several great battles, in which archers and cannon played a part. However, the final victory fell to the king of France, Charles VII, whose armies were led by the young shepherdess from Lorraine known as Joan of Arc. The war was damaging to France. Soldiers, who were rarely paid, roamed in "Great Companies," pillaging villages, killing livestock, robbing peasants, burning houses and massacring anyone who resisted.

At the end of the 12th century, Europe was prosperous. Yet, in the 14th century, all the advances made were put at risk by famines, epidemics and wars. Despite this, the formation of the European states continued.

The growth of the towns

The population increased all across Europe in the 13th century, growing from about 45 million in the 11th century to 75 million in the middle of the 14th century. The living conditions of peasants improved as a result of developments in agriculture. People ate better and more. They had more resistance to disease and lived longer. The increase in the population caused towns to grow. Artisans who manufactured goods such as cloth, weapons, pottery and jewelry grouped together in guilds or corporations. Each year, merchants from various countries met at great fairs such as those in Champagne and in Flanders. The richest merchants came from Genoa and Venice in Italy and from the Hanseatic league, a trading association of German towns. New wealth enabled towns to break free from dependence on lords. Belltowers, rising above city hall, were symbols of the cities' independence. In the growing towns, cathedrals were important buildings. Generations of carpenters, stonemasons and master glaziers toiled over

Paying rents to the lord's representative in the 15th century. ▼

Peasants in revolt during the 14th century.

Burial of plague victims in Tournai, modern Belgium, during the Black Death in 1349. ▲

their construction. Royalty and bishops sponsored the setting up of universities. The first were founded in the 12th century in Italy (Bologna) and France (Paris), after which the movement extended to the rest of Europe, to England (Oxford and Cambridge), Spain (Seville) and central Europe (Cracow, Vienna).

Calamities of the times

Prosperity ended in the 14th century. The population had outgrown the food supply. Epidemics reappeared. The most terrible of these was the Black Death, which killed more than a quarter of the European population between 1347 and 1353. Conflicts also multiplied, among them the Hundred Years' War between France and England (1337-1453), and the Wars of the Roses (1455-1485) in England. Revolts broke out in the countryside and towns and were harshly put down. Religious Europe was also divided. From 1309, following a quarrel between French bishops and the papacy, two popes were elected at the same time—one in Rome and the other at Avignon in France. This situation lasted until 1377.

The birth of European states

Wars with their neighbors inspired a feeling of solidarity and unity in peoples. They also strengthened the attachment to ruling dynasties, whether to Capetians in France, the Catholic kings in Spain or the kings of Portugal. In central Europe, new kingdoms emerged: Bohemia, Hungary, Poland and Russia. These countries had to confront enemies from the west, the Teutonic knights of German origin and from the east, the Mongols and Turks. In the north, the kingdoms of Sweden, Norway and Denmark united or fought with each other by turns. Princes reigned in Burgundy and Flanders and in the many small states and free cities that made up what are now Italy and Germany. In Spain, the *Reconquista*, or reconquest of territories from the Moors (Muslims), was completed with the capture of Granada in 1492. In the 15th century a new era—the Renaissance—began in Italy, where princes who governed city-states were patrons of artists and scientists. At the same time, navigators from Spain and Portugal set out in search of the "new world." □

◄ **A Teutonic knight.**

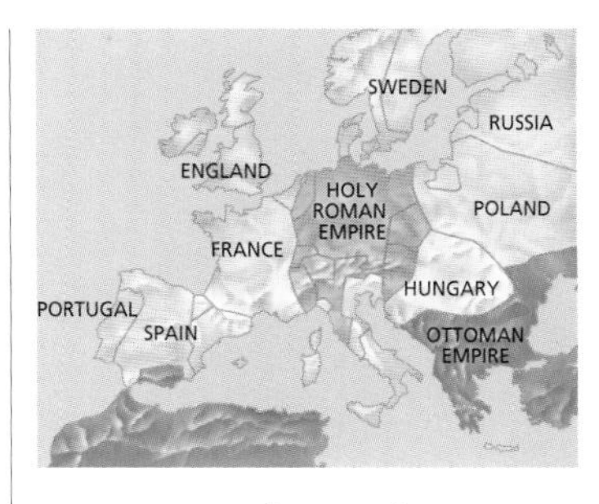

Europe at the end of the Middle Ages ▲

England, Spain and France, still important nations within Europe, are among the states shown.

View of the port of Bruges

The port of Bruges in Flanders is linked to the sea by canals. Wines from France and Spain, silks from Venice, English wool and Scandinavian timber were traded here. The town also had industries such as weaving. Merchants employed workers to weave English wool, and they became so rich that they could lend money to the king. ▼

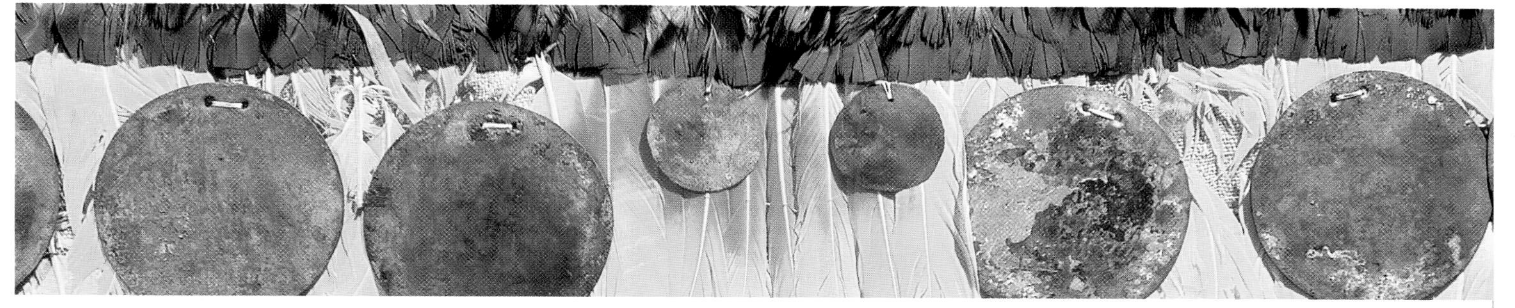

A costume of feathers and gold plates from Peru, 13th-14th centuries.

were wiped out after the settlement of Europeans.

The Olmecs and the Mayas

The oldest cities known in the Americas are in the south of present-day Mexico, where two peoples lived who both worshipped the jaguar-god: the Olmecs, before 1000 BC, followed by the Mayas until the 10th century AD. The Olmecs built monumental sculptures and were probably responsible for the knowledge of astronomy and calendars later refined by the Mayas. The Mayas built more than a hundred cities, each of which dominated the surrounding countryside as a small state. They also set up pyramids with temples on top where they worshipped half-man, half-animal gods and the jaguar-god. Rulers lived in single-story palaces with many rooms arranged around a central courtyard.

The Aztecs

The Aztecs came originally from southern Mexico, where their Toltec ancestors had lived. A conquering people, the Aztecs settled in the Valley of Mexico during the 14th century and built their capital, Tenochtitlán. In the 14th century, their empire stretched from the Atlantic to the Pacific. Aztec society was divided into several classes. At the top were the warriors and the priests; then came the merchants, followed by the peasants; at the bottom of the social scale were the servants and slaves. Like the Toltecs, the Aztecs worshiped the Feathered Serpent, a god also known as Quetzalcoatl. To honor the gods, they made human sacrifices, and for this reason, they were feared by neighboring peoples, who were forced to supply captives for sacrifices. The Aztecs grew corn, beans, melons, vanilla, tomatoes, several types of cotton and tobacco. Their merchants (*pochtecas*) brought products from all parts of America. Trade was by exchange of precious objects made of jade and turquoise, bird's feathers and cocoa beans.

The Incas

In the Andes of South America, various peoples in the 14th century came under the domination of the Incas. This people took their name from their emperor, the Inca, priest of the sun-god and himself worshiped like the sun. The emperor's capital was at Cuzco in Peru, and his orders were sent throughout the empire by messengers who used the "roads of the Inca." The Incas built monumental cities such as Machu Picchu, dating from the middle of the 15th century, which served them as a refuge during the Spanish conquest. The people were divided into clans (*ayllu*) and lived by farming, producing corn, potatoes and a cereal, quinoa. Taxes were paid in blankets, usually made of feathers. Writing was unknown and the Incas kept their accounts with a system of knotted strings, known as quipu. □

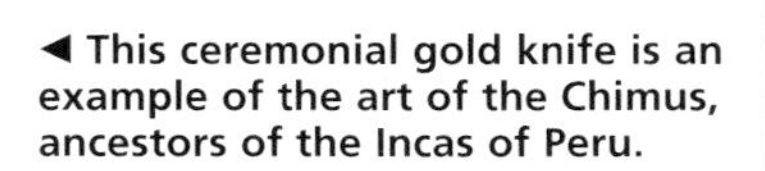

◀ This ceremonial gold knife is an example of the art of the Chimus, ancestors of the Incas of Peru.

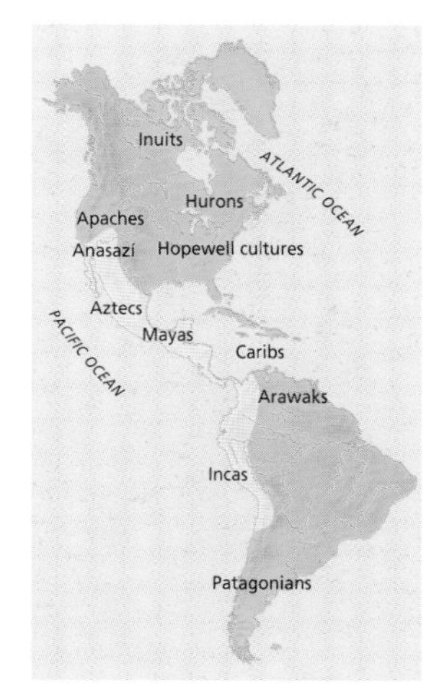

The peoples of the Americas ▲

Most peoples of North America were nomadic. In the south, great empires formed.

The king of Texcoco

Nezahualcoyotl (1402-1472) was a powerful ally of the Aztecs. Like them, he wore sumptuous robes of feathers. ▼

new

worlds

The 15th and 16th centuries saw a dramatic increase in the number of long-distance voyages made by Portuguese and Spanish sailors and explorers. Europeans were soon to conquer enormous territories.

The discoveries

1430 Prince Henry the Navigator of Portugal launches the first expeditions to explore the African coasts.
1487 Bartolomeu Dias rounds the Cape of Good Hope.
1492 The expedition led by Christopher Columbus discovers the West Indies, islands close to the American mainland.
1494 The Spanish and Portuguese divide the New World by the Treaty of Tordesillas.
1498 The navigator Vasco da Gama rounds Africa and reaches India.
1499-1502 Amerigo Vespucci explores the coasts of South America.
1521 Hernando Cortes defeats the Aztec Empire and conquers Mexico.
1522 The expedition led by Ferdinand Magellan completes the first voyage around the world.
1533 Francisco Pizarro takes Cuzco in Peru and ends the Inca Empire.
1534-1535 Jacques Cartier takes possession of Canada and sails up the St. Lawrence River.
1584 Sir Walter Raleigh founds a colony which he names Virginia (modern-day North Carolina).

▲ A ship of the Age of Discoveries: a model of a 16th-century Portuguese ship.

Curiosity, advances in navigation, the desire to discover new riches and the determination to convert other peoples to Christianity encouraged 15th-century Europeans to set off on great expeditions across the sea. Such voyages were made possible by the support of the Portuguese and Spanish kings, among others. By the end of the century, Europeans were to be found in most parts of the world.

The Portuguese

Around the year 1430, Henry, son of the king of Portugal, dreamed of distant lands. Their discovery would mean that Europeans would no longer have to buy spices, silk and other goods at exorbitant prices from the Arab merchants who controlled trade with India and China. Prince Henry, known as "the Navigator," tried to open a new trade route to these countries by sea, around the southern tip of Africa. He assembled scholars and sailors to explore the African coasts systematically. Their great discoveries were made possible by technical innovations such as the new ships called caravels, with sails that could withstand storms well, and by the drawing of more accurate maritime charts called portolans. During the first half of the 15th century, the Portuguese discovered the Atlantic islands, the Azores and the Canaries; they followed the African coast to Senegal and then to Guinea where they established trading posts. However, for a long time it seemed that no route to the Far East was there to be discovered. Finally in 1487, a captain named Bartolomeu Dias sailed as far south as the tip of southern Africa, later named the Cape of Good Hope. The route to the Indies was now open for the Portuguese. In 1498, Vasco da Gama became the first European navigator to round Africa and reach India by sea.

Jacques Cartier going up the St. Lawrence River in Canada.

The Spanish

Like their Portuguese neighbors, the Spanish kings dreamed of gold and spices. Christopher Columbus, an explorer originally from Genoa in Italy, set before them a plan to cross the Atlantic Ocean and reach the Indies (Asia) from the west. In 1492, he set out in command of three ships that reached land after 43 days at sea. Columbus thought that he had arrived in India. He had in fact discovered the West Indies, islands close to America. Columbus took possession of these lands for Spain and called the people of the islands "Indians." In 1498, he reached the American mainland in present-day Venezuela. Other explorers followed him. One, Amerigo Vespucci, explored the coasts of South America, and the continent was named America in his honor. Expeditions multiplied and advances in navigation made another exploit possible: between 1519 and 1522, a Spanish expedition led by the Portuguese navigator Ferdinand Magellan and completed after Magellan's death by his second-in-command made the first voyage around the world.

Battle between Indians and Spanish conquistadors in the 16th century. ▼

The first conquests

After discoveries came conquests. From the beginning of the 16th century the Spanish launched military expeditions to take possession of the newly discovered lands. The soldiers who went with them were known as *conquistadors*, conquerors. In 1521, Hernando Cortes brought down the Aztec Empire and seized Mexico. From 1531 to 1533, Francisco Pizarro conquered Peru and ended the Inca Empire. Other conquistadors took possession of Colombia, Bolivia and Florida. Thousands of Indians died in battles or became victims of diseases brought by the conquerors. The Spanish and Portuguese tried to keep the new lands for themselves. However, the English, Dutch and French sent out expeditions of their own, and from 1600, East India Companies were set up to organize trade with distant lands. The Dutch established themselves in Java and the other Indonesian islands. The French and English chose the Atlantic route and tried to find a northern passage to the Indies. But they encountered only the seemingly endless coastline of North America. In 1534, the French sailor Jacques Cartier took possession of Canada on behalf of the king of France. In 1584, Sir Walter Raleigh founded a colony that he named Virginia (in present-day North Carolina), in the honor of Queen Elizabeth of England. This was the beginning of European settlement in North America. □

Ferdinand Magellan ▲
This Portuguese explorer was the first to prove that the Earth is round. He left Spain in 1519 with 5 ships and 265 men, followed the South American coast and crossed the Pacific Ocean. He landed in the Philippines where he was killed. His second-in-command returned to Spain with 18 men.

Jacques Cartier
This French explorer searched the northwest Atlantic for a route to the Indies and China. He landed in Canada in 1534. ▼

From the 15th to the 18th centuries, Europe underwent great artistic, religious and political changes. Historians call this period the modern era, because it opens the way to our contemporary world.

Europe

1494-1559 The Italian wars: the Renaissance spreads throughout Europe.
1509 England: beginning of the reign of Henry VIII.
1517 Germany: start of the Protestant Reformation.
1519 Charles V becomes emperor of the Holy Roman Empire.
1545-1563 Italy: Council of Trent, which prepares the Counter-Reformation.
1555 Germany: Peace of Augsburg, ending the wars of religion.
1581 Netherlands: formation of the United Provinces.
1598 France: the Edict of Nantes gives freedom of worship to Protestants. End of the French wars of religion.
1643-1715 France: reign of Louis XIV.
1649 England: Charles I is executed. Oliver Cromwell heads the Commonwealth.
1660 England: restoration of the monarchy.
1682 Russia: Peter the Great becomes tsar.
1689 England: King William of Orange accepts the Bill of Rights imposed by Parliament.

In the Middle Ages, cultural and intellectual life in Europe was strictly controlled by the Church. In the 15th and 16th centuries, the Renaissance (meaning "rebirth") transformed Christian Europe. This cultural and artistic movement was stimulated by renewed links with the learning of ancient Greece and Rome and led to a break with the traditions of the Middle Ages. The Protestant Reformation divided Christians and led to religious wars.

Renaissance and humanism

The Renaissance began in Italy in the 15th century. Italy was a patchwork of states formed of cities such as Florence, Milan, Venice and Rome, which had become rich through trade. In Florence, the Medici family of powerful bankers surrounded themselves with a lavish court. Like other similar rulers, they built palaces and employed artists whom they protected and supported financially. One example was the painter Michelangelo. Another was the architect, painter and scientist Leonardo da Vinci. Such patrons made it possible for new art to flourish. The Renaissance revolutionized ways of thinking and artistic life. Artists admired Greek and Roman works and were inspired by them. Scholars studied the texts of the great authors of the ancient world, translating them from Greek and Latin into their own languages. A new current of thought, known as humanism, developed in Europe. The humanists questioned a number of ideas, including those of religion. Their interest in the sciences led them to study humanity and nature.

◄ A Renaissance sculpture made in 15th-century Florence.

A new political map

Between 1494 and 1559, France and Spain fought in Italy to gain possession of the Italian states. The Hapsburg family, which had reigned over Austria since the 13th century, extended its rule to other countries in the 15th century as a result of various inheritances. It gained the Holy Roman Empire (roughly modern Germany), part of Italy and the Netherlands. When the Spanish ruler Charles V became emperor in 1519, he added Spain and its American colonies to the Empire. In England, Henry VII ended the civil wars known as the Wars of the Roses in 1485 and restored unity to the kingdom. His son, Henry VIII, succeeded him in 1509.

The Reformation

In 1517, a German monk named Martin Luther denounced the abuses then rife in the Christian Church. He set off a reform movement that spread rapidly through the

Massacres and looting in 1562 during the French wars of religion.

Holy Roman Empire and then over a large part of Europe. This reformation led to a new Christian movement, Protestantism, which was opposed to the authority of the Catholic Church in Rome (see *Religions of the World*). The pope reacted by convening an assembly of Catholic bishops, the Council of Trent (1545-1563). This assembly decided to reform the Catholic Church and so led to a movement known as the Counter-Reformation. The Reformation and Counter-Reformation involved violent conflicts between supporters of the two movements.

▲ **Martin Luther preaching.**

The wars of religion

The Holy Roman Empire, which was made up of separate states grouped under the authority of the emperor, Charles V, was divided between Catholics and Protestants. War broke out. The war was ended by the Peace of Augsburg in 1555. In France, Protestantism, spread by John Calvin, expanded rapidly. Religious conflicts tore the kingdom apart as Catholics and Protestants fought to impose their faith on the other. Henry IV, a Protestant who was willing to accept Catholicism, restored peace. In 1598, this French king issued the Edict of Nantes, which gave Protestants freedom to practice their religion. England joined the religious struggle following a conflict between Henry VIII and the pope over the king's divorce. In 1533, Henry VIII proclaimed himself head of the Church of England, which became Protestant. □

Prince Lorenzo de' Medici (1449-1492), a wealthy Italian patron of the arts. ▼

The invention of printing

Shown below is a printer's workshop, around 1520. The workers, a printing press and tools can be seen.

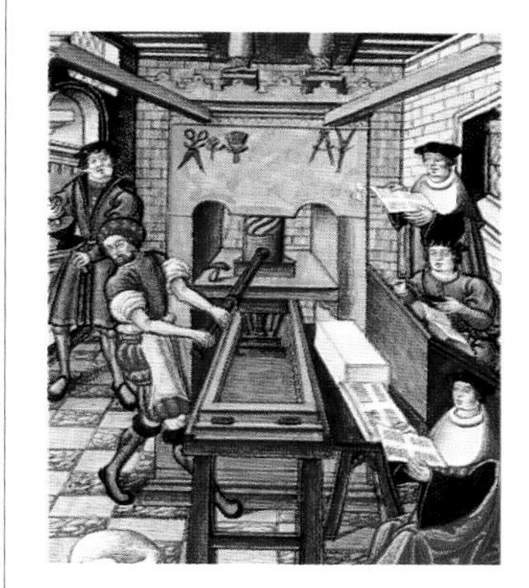

A German called Johannes Gutenberg invented printing using movable type. Gutenberg perfected letters made from lead, which could be moved and rearranged to form any word. The letters or characters were first arranged on a plate, then coated with ink and applied to a sheet of parchment or paper by a strong screw press. Once the page was made up (composed), hundreds could be printed. Books before this time had been copied by hand. They now became much less costly and therefore within reach of far more people. Printing was the main reason for the rapid spread of knowledge throughout Europe.

King Louis XIV of France and his court, about 1690.

The 17th century

The siege of Vienna in 1683 ▲

From the 15th century, the Turks controlled Asia Minor and a part of Europe. Their fleet was feared throughout the Mediterranean. In the 16th century, they extended their empire into Eastern Europe. The Hapsburg rulers of Spain and Austria resisted the Turks, who were defeated at the sea battle of Lepanto in 1571. Turkish armies twice laid siege to Vienna, in 1529 and again in 1683.

In the 17th century, the model of government in a number of European countries was the absolute monarchy, as in France under Louis XIV. Other countries, such as England, evolved toward a system of constitutional monarchy, in which a parliament shared power with the king. This century was also the age of great artists such as the playwrights Shakespeare in England and La Fontaine and Molière in France, and the painter Rembrandt in Holland.

France, the model for absolute monarchy

Richelieu, the counselor of France's king Louis XIII, concentrated all power in the hands of the king and compelled the nobility to obey him. This type of government came to be known as absolute monarchy, and during the reign of Louis XIV, the system, which was to last 150 years, became fully established. Several European monarchies, including Russia and Sweden, took France as their model. After 1661, Louis XIV governed personally. He reorganized the administration of the kingdom, created numerous institutions and reinforced his authority through civil servants called intendants, who represented the king in the provinces. With the help of his minister Colbert, the king developed overseas trade that enriched France and increased its power. He had the Palace of Versailles built as a royal residence and moved the court there in 1682. Louis XIV, known as the Sun-King, enjoyed immense prestige in Europe.

A middle-class family of the Netherlands. ▼

England moves toward a constitutional monarchy

Until the end of the 17th century, the history of England was marked by conflicts between the king and parliament, which was attempting to widen its powers. Parliament was an assembly that the monarch needed to approve laws and raise taxes, thus checking royal power. Charles I, who reigned from 1625, tried to rule in an absolute manner, and this led to parliament's revolt in 1642. Civil war broke out. Oliver Cromwell, a member of parliament, became a leader of its army, which defeated the royalists. The king was taken prisoner and executed in 1649. Cromwell set up a republican-style government, dominated by Protestant extremists called Puritans, who attempted to impose on society an austere moral code. Ireland and Scotland rebelled, after which Cromwell instituted a military dictatorship. He died in 1658. In 1660, Charles II restored the monarchy but parliament continued to defend its rights against arbitrary decisions of the king. When James II, a Catholic who became king in 1685, tried to bring back absolutism, he was deposed. In 1689, the English parliament offered the crown jointly to James's daughter Mary and her husband William of Orange, a Protestant prince of the Netherlands, but

The execution of Charles I of England in 1649.

passed the Bill of Rights, which defined the powers of the king. England had become a constitutional monarchy.

The other European states

Not all the countries of Europe were monarchies. Switzerland was divided into cantons, which joined in a confederation and achieved independence from the Holy Roman Empire in 1499. The Holy Roman Empire, governed by the Hapsburg dynasty, was made up of more than 300 states that included monarchies such as Bavaria and Saxony, the Duchy of Prussia and towns such as Hamburg and Bremen. The Hapsburgs had much more power over Austria, Hungary and Bohemia, which they controlled directly. Absolute monarchy failed to take hold in the Netherlands, where the commercial strength of the country allowed the rich middle class to play a significant political role. In 1581, the Protestant provinces of the Netherlands declared independence from the Hapsburgs and formed a confederation of seven republics, the United Provinces. The United Provinces were ruled by an assembly of representatives from each province, dominated by Holland. □

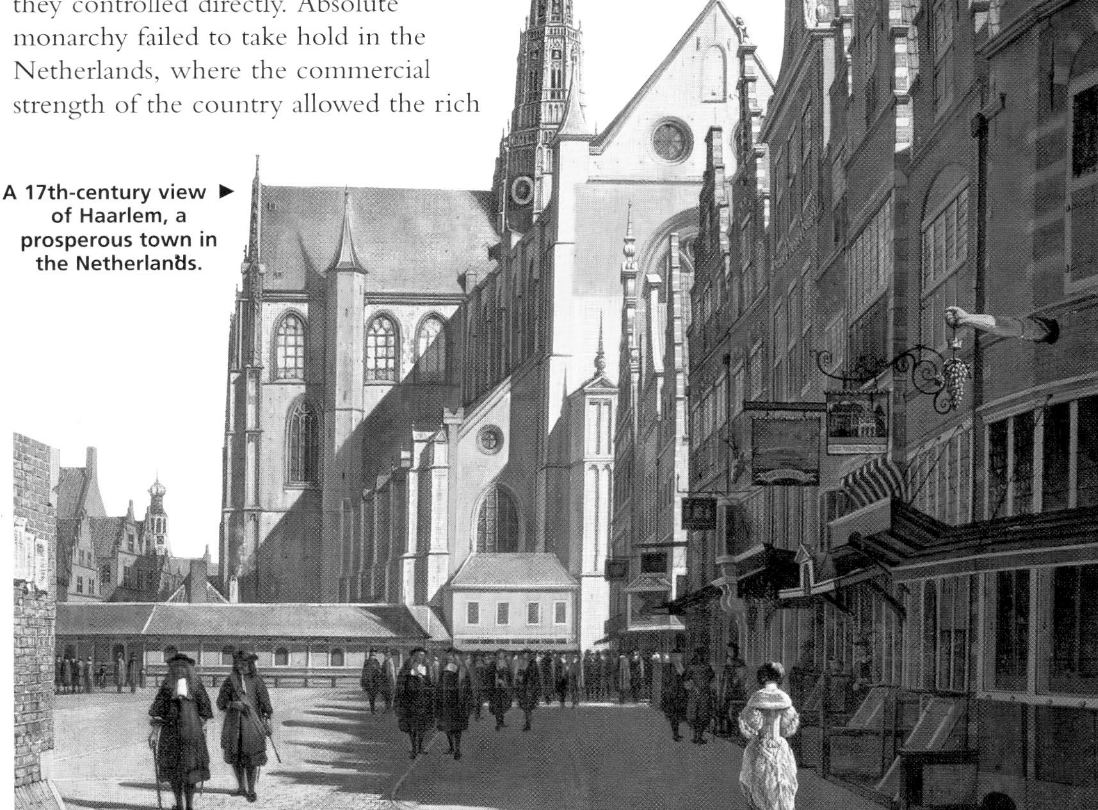
A 17th-century view ► of Haarlem, a prosperous town in the Netherlands.

The Thirty Years War

The Thirty Years War took place from 1618 to 1648 between the Holy Roman Empire (governed by the Hapsburg family), Denmark, Sweden and France. The war began because the Catholic Hapsburgs wanted to limit the power of the Protestant Germanic states that were part of their Empire. The Hapsburgs were supported by Denmark, followed by Sweden and then France.

The war was devastating. It destroyed large parts of the Germanic states and the west of France.

The emperor of the Holy Roman Empire was finally forced to sign the treaty of Westphalia in 1648, ending the war. Under this treaty the Germanic states of the Holy Roman Empire had much more independence than before the war, a fact that the empire was forced to accept when it signed the agreement.

The 18th century witnessed a new style of government known as "enlightened despotism." These liberal ideas paved the way for the creation of the United States and the French Revolution.

The 18th century—the

1703 Peter the Great, tsar (emperor) of Russia, founds St. Petersburg.
1740-1786 Reign of Frederick II (the Great) of Prussia.
1745-1780 Maria Theresa, empress of Austria.
1750-1753 Voltaire, the French philosopher, lives at the court of Frederick of Prussia.
1751-1772 Publication of the Encyclopédie by Diderot and d'Alembert.
1762-1796 Catherine II, empress of Russia.
1762-1790 Joseph II, emperor of Austria.
1773-1774 Russia: the Pugachev revolt against serfdom.

The 18th century is known as the Age of Reason or Enlightenment, because the thinkers of this period believed that advances of the human mind "enlightened" humanity. In France and later in all of Europe, a new ideal of society spread, based on knowledge, religious tolerance and liberty. These ideas won over some European rulers who tried to apply them in their states.

The century of reason and liberty

In the 18th century in Europe, science and technology made great progress, following in the footsteps of 17th-century scientists such as Newton, who had explained gravity. Buffon described all the known species of animals, and Jenner pioneered vaccination.

▼ Frederick II of Prussia and a courtier at the Sans-Souci Palace, Potsdam.

This was the era of the steam engine and of the first steam vehicles. Thinkers, such as the French writers and philosophers Montesquieu and Voltaire, criticized the abuses of absolute monarchy. In France, a group of scholars and writers, headed by Denis Diderot and Jean d'Alembert, decided to bring together in a single volume all human knowledge. This became the *Encyclopédie*, published from 1751 to 1772. A gigantic work, it covered everything from wig making to the role of the king to freedom of religion. The *Encyclopédie* called many accepted ideas into question. From France, the publication spread throughout Europe and became a tool for widespread investigation and reflection. Philosophers and scholars defended freedom of thought and searched for truth by relying on reason, in other words, on observation and analysis. The ideas of the Enlightenment were widely discussed in the courts and salons of Europe and were taken up by a number of rulers who are known as "enlightened despots."

Prussia and Austria, modern states

Prussia was one of the kingdoms of the Holy Roman Empire. At the beginning of the 18th century, King Frederick William I (1688-1740) turned it into a powerful state, equipped with a well-trained army. His son Frederick II (1712–1786) used this force to impose his will, so that Prussia became the principal power of the empire. As an enlightened despot, he dreamed of transforming his country. He had roads and canals built, villages founded and marshes drained. He improved its agriculture and introduced the potato to combat famines. He was very authoritarian and saw to it that the same justice was applied to all the Prussians, whether noble, middle class or peasant. All

Writers and encyclopedists meet at an 18th-century literary salon.

Enlightenment

Vienna in the 18th century: the Austrian city was the Hapsburg capital.

enjoyed freedom of religion. Frederick II of Prussia surrounded himself with artists, and invited the radical writer Voltaire to his palace, Sans-Souci.
In Austria, Empress Maria Theresa and later her son Joseph II undertook important reforms, for example in education and the fairer distribution of taxes. Again, religious diversity was tolerated. But the different traditions and origins of their subjects (Austrians, Slovaks, Hungarians and others) hindered the efforts of the rulers. Enlightened reforms proved difficult to apply.

Reforms in Russia

In the 18th century, Russia was governed by two "enlightened despots" who attempted to turn their backward country into a modern state. Before becoming tsar, Peter the Great traveled across Europe. On his return, he reformed the government and the army. He founded and built his future capital, St. Petersburg, which became a great port for Russia, opening onto the Baltic Sea and so to the West. Beginning in 1762, Catherine II continued Peter the Great's work. She increased Russia's power by conquering the Crimea, taken from the Turks in 1771. Her favorite, Prince Potemkin, in 1775 reorganized the country's administration, promoted trade and encouraged the nobles to form trading companies. An admirer of the ideas of the Enlightenment philosophers, Catherine II, known as Catherine the Great, founded schools and promoted education. However, these reforms did not reach the poorest section of the population, the peasants. The number of Russian peasants reduced to serfdom (attached like property to an estate with no right to leave) increased during her reign. In 1773-1774, a revolt led by Pugachev united the warlike Cossack horsemen from Russia's borders with peasants who demanded the abolition of serfdom. □

Change in Russia

"The war against beards" depicts Peter the Great, tsar of Russia, cutting the beard of one of his nobles. The wearing of beards was traditional among the Orthodox Christians of Russia, but the tsar wanted his subjects to look like Westerners, considering the beard an attachment to the past. At first beards were heavily taxed and then bearded men were obliged to shave, under pain of death. Among those who most resolutely opposed the tsar's reforms were the Old Believers. In 1666-1667, these conservative Christians were excluded from the Russian Orthodox Church because they did not accept the reforms that it had adopted. ▼

An English family

Pictured here are the children of a well-to-do, middle-class Englishman named Daniel Graham. This portrait was made by a celebrated 18th-century painter named Hogarth. Before this time, only the children of kings or nobles were considered worthy of being painted. But in the 18th century, children began to play a much larger role in the life of the family. During this same period, sovereigns throughout Europe were building huge palaces inspired by the French castle of Versailles, like the Russian one pictured here, near St. Petersburg.

Europeans settled in North America from the 17th century, founding the first colonies. In the 18th century, a group of British colonies became independent and gave birth to the United States.

Birth of the United

The first Europeans settled in North America in the 17th century and founded the first colonies. More than a century later, in 1775, the British colonies rebelled in a war of independence that led to the formation of a new nation—the United States of America.

The thirteen English colonies

Sir Walter Raleigh founded the first English colonial settlement in America in 1584. Raleigh's colony was unsuccessful, and the first parliament settlement by the English, Jamestown, was made in 1607. The English, Swedes, Dutch and French gradually settled on the Atlantic coast of the North American continent. In 1620, a group of strict Protestants called Puritans left England on a ship named the *Mayflower* to seek religious freedom in America. Known today as the Pilgrims, they founded the colony of Plymouth and later, Massachusetts. People in the United States continue to commemorate Thanksgiving Day, which the colonists first celebrated a year after their arrival. In 1683, the rich idealist William Penn founded Pennsylvania and its capital of Philadelphia, the City of Brotherly Love. The English colonies were founded separately from each other. By the middle of the 18th century, there were thirteen colonies, all ruled by the British parliament but increasingly concerned with self-government.

The French in North America

The French began to settle in Canada, discovered by Jacques Cartier in the 16th century. Many were attracted to the possibilities offered by this territory, including exploitation of new and potentially rich lands and trade in furs with the Indians. Samuel de Champlain founded the city of Quebec in 1608, and gradually the French moved into the interior. They settled on the shores of the Great Lakes and founded Detroit.

Landing in 1620 of the Pilgrims, some of the first colonists in America.

- **1584** Sir Walter Raleigh founds the first English colony in North America.
- **1608** Samuel de Champlain founds the city of Quebec in Canada.
- **1620** The Pilgrims arrive in America on board the *Mayflower*.
- **1682** Cavelier de La Salle explores the Mississippi and claims Louisiana.
- **1683** William Penn founds the colony of Pennsylvania.
- **18th c.** Thirteen British colonies in North America.
- **1718** The French found New Orleans in Louisiana.
- **1763** End of the Seven Years' War between France and Britain: Canada becomes British.
- **1775** Beginning of the Revolutionary War between the American colonists and Britain.
- **1776** Declaration of Independence by the 13 American states.
- **1783** Britain recognizes the independence of its colonies in America.
- **1787** Proclamation of the Constitution of the United States of America.
- **1789** George Washington is elected president of the United States.

Monticello, the home in Virginia of Thomas Jefferson, third President of the United States.

States

Cavelier de La Salle explored the banks of the Mississippi, naming the area west of the river Louisiana, in honor of Louis XIV. The French also founded St. Louis and New Orleans.

Rivalries between the colonists

Europeans came into conflict in North America. Wars begun in Europe were also fought out in the colonies. In the mid-18th century there were 2 million British colonists in North America and only 54,000 French. The French and British fought the Seven Years' War (1756-1763) in Europe and in their colonies. The war ended with Britain victorious and with the French losing their territory in Canada.

The Revolutionary War and the birth of the United States

Britain's American colonies wanted greater autonomy. The colonists refused to pay taxes that they considered unjust, and in 1770 riots broke out in Boston. New ideas from Europe influenced the Americans, who spoke of independence. In 1774, the thirteen colonies decided to break off all trade with Britain. In 1775, war broke out. George Washington took command of the American troops against the British army. In 1776, Thomas Jefferson and Benjamin Franklin drafted the Declaration of Independence. France supported the American colonists, and French volunteers such as the Marquis de Lafayette joined them. In 1783, Britain recognized American independence in the Treaty of Paris. In 1787, the Constitution of the United States of America was adopted. It set up a republic with a president elected every four years. The Congress, an assembly divided into two chambers, the House of Representatives and the Senate, was to approve new laws. The United States formed a federal republic, and its member states held on to much of their power. The Revolutionary War and the emergence of a republic were to influence the French Revolution of 1789. □

General George Washington and the Marquis de Lafayette in 1777. ▼

George Washington ▲

In 1789, Washington was elected first president of the United States under the American Constitution, which founded the first great modern democracy, a political system in which power rests with the people.

Samuel de Champlain

An envoy of Henry IV, king of France, Samuel de Champlain set out in 1604 for New France (Canada), intending to convert the Indians to Christianity and to enlarge the royal dominions. He founded Port-Royal and Quebec and in 1619 became governor of Canada. ▼

In 1789, revolution broke out in France. Beginning there, the revolutionary movement spread to other European countries, which later endured invasion by the armies of Napoleon Bonaparte.

The French Revolution

1774 Louis XVI, king of France.
1789 Meeting of the Estates-General in France. Popular revolt in Paris and storming of the Bastille. Declaration of the Rights of Man and of the Citizen.
1792 Battle of Valmy: the armies of Prussia and Austria are defeated by the French. This marks the beginning of the wars between France and other European countries. Proclamation of the French Republic.
1793 Louis XVI is sentenced to death and guillotined. The Reign of Terror in France until 1794.
1804 Napoleon Bonaparte is crowned emperor.
1805 Naval battle of Trafalgar: victory for Britain over France. Battle of Austerlitz: French victory over the Austrians and Russians.
1806 Prussia is defeated by France. Berlin is occupied by the French.
1812 The French are defeated by the Russians.
1815 Battle of Waterloo: finally defeated, Napoleon surrenders to the British. The allies occupy Paris. The Congress of Vienna reorganizes the whole of Europe.

In 1789, revolution ended the absolute monarchy in France. Revolutionary fervor then spread to other European countries. From 1792 to 1815, European monarchies fought first against the spread of revolution and then against the conquests of Napoleon.

The French Revolution

In 1789, to solve the financial difficulties of France, Louis XVI called together the Estates-General, an assembly with representatives from the nobility, the clergy and the third estate (middle classes and peasants). This last group demanded reforms and questioned the absolute monarchy. On 14 July 1789, a popular revolt broke out: Parisians stormed the prison of the Bastille, a symbol of royal authority. In August, the Estates-General declared itself a National Constituent Assembly. It adopted the Declaration of the Rights of Man and of the Citizen, which expressed the revolutionary ideal of liberty and equality for all. In 1791, a constitutional monarchy was set up by which the king was to rule with a legislative assembly to approve laws. Absolute monarchy was at an end. The other European monarchies, alarmed by these events, went to war with France, while in that country itself, royalists and revolutionaries clashed. In 1792, the French republic was proclaimed. The king of France was tried and, in 1793, executed, and a dictatorship was set up. This Reign of Terror—so called because of the numbers of opponents of the revolution who were executed—lasted until 1794. In 1795, power was invested in five directors in a government known as the Directory.

Storming of the Bastille in Paris, 14 July 1789. ▼

British victory at the battle of Trafalgar in 1805.

and Europe

Napoleon and Alexander I, tsar of Russia.

The Revolution spreads

Revolutionary upheavals then occurred in Geneva (Switzerland), the Low Countries (in what is now Belgium) and Italy. France presented itself as the defender of liberty and, regarding the Alps and the Rhine as its natural frontiers, set out to conquer neighboring countries in the name of freedom. Wars were waged from 1792 to 1815. In countries conquered by the French armies, small republics on the French model were proclaimed. In 1795, the Batavian Republic was set up in Holland, the Helvetian Republic in Switzerland and the Republic of Rome in Italy. To oppose the French armies, Prussia, Austria, Spain, Britain and the Netherlands joined in alliance. From this date, warring armies were not just professional soldiers but also peoples struggling for the recognition of their national identity. Following a string of successful military campaigns, the general Napoleon Bonaparte became highly popular in France. In 1799, he replaced the Directory with the Consulate, consisting of three consuls. Bonaparte himself was first consul. In 1804, he had himself crowned emperor.

Napoleon and Europe

From 1804 to 1815, Napoleon fought the European countries allied against France. Although Britain won the sea battle of Trafalgar in 1805, the French armies made deep inroads in Europe. The Austrians and the Russians were defeated at the battle of Austerlitz in 1805; Austria was again defeated at Wagram in 1809. Napoleon became master of Europe. Only Britain continued to resist. The emperor reorganized the conquered states, imposing new forms of government on them. In 1806, the Holy Roman Empire was dissolved and the Confederation of the Rhine, a union of the German states, was set up. Some peoples resisted French domination, in particular the Spanish from 1808. In 1812, Napoleon's armies were forced to retreat from Russia. Two years later, France was invaded by European armies and Napoleon abdicated. After a period of exile on the island of Elba he returned to power in France but was finally defeated at the battle of Waterloo in 1815. □

The Congress of Vienna in 1815

After Napoleon's final defeat, representatives of the victorious allies—Russia, Prussia, Austria and Britain—met in 1815 in Vienna, Austria, for a peace conference. The Congress marked the end of the Napoleonic wars and was designed to weaken France. It dismantled the Napoleonic empire and reorganized Europe. From this point, the principal European powers were Britain, Austria, Prussia and Russia. Germany and Italy remained divided. In France, the monarchy was restored with King Louis XVIII. However, the Congress of Vienna did not take into account the national aspirations of many peoples. ▼

The China of the Ming and Qing and the India of the Great Moguls were powerful empires in the 18th century. Diverse cultural influences, including Western, mingled. Only Japan refused to deal with the Europeans.

Asia

1409 China: Beijing becomes the capital of the Ming dynasty. Building of the Forbidden City, the palace of the emperor.

15th c. India: the Portuguese set up trading posts in Goa.

1526 India: founding of the Mogul dynasty in Delhi.

1556-1605 India: reign of the Mogul emperor Akbar.

1557 China: the Portuguese establish a trading post in Macao.

1582 Japan: end of the civil wars.

1600 India: Britain establishes its East India Company.

1603 Japan: the chief of the Tokugawa clan proclaims himself hereditary shogun and founds a dynasty. Edo becomes the capital of Japan.

1639 European merchants are no longer permitted to enter Japan, apart from the island of Deshima.

1644 China: end of the Ming dynasty. Accession of the Manchu dynasty of the Qing.

1658-1707 India: reign of the Mogul emperor Aurangzeb.

1661-1722 China: reign of the emperor Kangxi.

New dynasties came to power in 18th-century China, Japan and India, and under their influence, the Asian empires were transformed. While China and India tolerated the presence of European traders or religious missionaries, Japan remained closed to outside influences.

The Chinese emperor Kangxi (1654-1722).

China

From the 14th to the 18th centuries, two dynasties, the Ming and then the Qing, dominated the history of China. Under the Ming (1368-1644), China was divided into 13 provinces. Beijing became its capital in 1409 and there the Ming built lavish palaces, including the imperial palace. Since this was an area reserved for the emperor and his court alone, it was known as the Forbidden City. Artists produced precious objects, including the famous Ming porcelain. In the 16th century, Europeans established a presence in China: Portuguese merchants settled in Macao; Jesuit missionaries, sent to spread Christianity, were authorized to travel around China by the emperor. To protect itself from invasions threatening the north of the empire, the government restored the Great Wall. However, in the 17th century, the Manchus from north of China crossed the Great Wall, occupied Beijing and made themselves masters of the entire empire. This invasion in 1644 marked the end of the Ming dynasty. A Manchu, Shunzhi, became emperor of China and founded the Qing dynasty. Under his rule, the Manchus kept the Chinese out of power although later Manchu and Chinese cultures blended. The emperor Kangxi, who reigned from 1662 to 1722, was a learned Manchu who admired Chinese culture. At the death of emperor Qianlong, in 1796, the Chinese empire had expanded to include Burma and Tibet.

Japan

From the 12th century, power in Japan was shared between the emperor and the shogun, the head of the most powerful clan. During the 16th century, the country was ravaged by civil wars. Rival lords (or daimyos), surrounded by their

Portuguese merchants in 17th-century Japan. ▶

Detail of a Japanese folding screen: it shows the arrival of the Portuguese in 16th-century Japan.

samurai (warriors), fought fiercely. The shogun had practically no power. In 1582, Toyotomi Hideyoshi, the emperor's prime minister, subjugated the daimyos and put an end to the civil wars. In 1603, Ieyasu Tokugawa proclaimed himself hereditary shogun and founded a dynasty. He restored the military government, the *bakufu*, and brought the country to peace. The Tokugawa governed Japan from their capital at Edo. The lords had to follow a very strict code of conduct, the *bushido*. A new way of living developed among the well-to-do townspeople, exemplified by kabuki theater. In 1639, Japan closed itself against Western influences: Christianity was forbidden and foreigners could no longer settle in the country. The only exception was a small group of Dutch merchants who were allowed to trade from near Nagasaki.

India under the Great Moguls

In the north of India, dynasties of Turkish origin held the throne of Delhi until 1526. At the beginning of the 16th century, the Moguls conquered northern India. They were Muslims from Central Asia who were also of Turkish origin. In 1526, Babur, the lord of Kabul in Afghanistan, won the battle of Panipat against the troops of the Sultan of Delhi and founded the dynasty of the Moguls. His grandson, Akbar, was the real architect of the empire. Tolerant in religious matters, Akbar allowed Hindus to occupy posts in the civil service and did away with the taxes imposed on non-Muslims. He invited artists and scholars to his court, mixing Indian and Persian cultures. The emperor Aurangzeb, who ruled from 1658 to 1707, reaffirmed the supremacy of Muslims over Hindus, and this led to revolts in the Indian provinces. Aurangzeb was a conqueror who extended Mogul control over the provinces of the east and south, Assam and the Deccan. However, he clashed with the Marathas, who defended Hindu traditions. After Aurangzeb's reign, Mogul power declined. Europeans, who had been in India since the 16th century, set up powerful trading companies which gave them economic and, subsequently, political control. □

The Taj Mahal ▲

The Taj Mahal, near Agra in India, is a mausoleum built from 1631 to 1641 by the emperor Shah Jahan in memory of his wife, Mumtaz Mahal.

The Portuguese in India

A Portuguese woman is seen here with her Indian maids. The Portuguese were the first Europeans to settle in India. They founded Goa and the port of Bombay in the 15th century. ▼

Africa and Oceania are immense continents that were largely unexplored before the 18th century. Well-established kingdoms existed in Africa, while in Oceania people lived in small groups, fishing and hunting.

Africa and Oceania

15th c. Renaissance of the Songhai Empire (Niger). Founding of the kingdom of Oyo (southern Nigeria). First trade contacts between the Portuguese and African kingdoms.
1517-1587 The Ottoman Turks occupy Egypt and then take control of present-day Algeria and Tunisia.
16th c. European trading posts proliferate on the African coasts. Beginning of the slave trade to America.
1554 Morocco: Saadi dynasty.
1578 Morocco: beginning of the reign of Sultan al-Mansur, "the Victorious."
1591 The Moroccans destroy the Songhai Empire in Niger.
1652 Southern Africa; Dutch colonists settle at the Cape.
1666 Morocco: Alawi dynasty.
1766-1769 Expedition of the French navigator Bougainville to Tahiti.
1768-1778 Captain James Cook of Britain makes three voyages of exploration in the Pacific Ocean.
1807 Britain prohibits the slave trade.
1815 France prohibits the slave trade.

Assembling captured slaves on a slave ship.

Through their trading activities, the peoples of North Africa extended their influence in black Africa and the Indian Ocean in the 16th century. In black Africa, large areas were controlled by well-organized kingdoms, some of which established links with European traders on the Atlantic coast. The deportation of black slaves to America was one result of such contacts. The Pacific lands of Oceania, populated by peoples who lived from hunting, gathering and fishing, remained unknown to Europeans until the 18th century.

North Africa

In the 16th century, the Turks of the Ottoman Empire conquered Egypt (1517) and the Maghreb (modern Algeria and Tunisia). These lands, which had been Muslim for 800 years, became provinces of the Ottoman Empire. Only Morocco kept its independence, under three successive dynasties: the Wattasid, the Saadi and then the Alawi from 1666. The Moroccans fought

◄ The ksar (fortress) of Tamdakht, in southern Morocco

Landing of Captain James Cook in the New Hebrides, in 1774.

off the Ottomans, as well as the Spanish and Portuguese. Sultan al-Mansur (Arabic for "the Victorious") traded with the Europeans and conquered the basin of the Niger River, south of the Sahara.

Black Africa

The powerful Songhai Empire, which controlled the upper Niger, was destroyed in the 16th century by the Moroccan conquest. However, other kingdoms endured elsewhere in Africa. In the south, near the Zambezi River, the kingdom of Monomotapa resisted the Portuguese, who were attracted by the richness of the country and by gold. In the west, several kingdoms, including Dahomey, Oyo and Ashanti, based their prosperity on trade with Europeans who established trading posts on the Atlantic coast. The main trade was in slaves, whom these kingdoms drew from the interior. They supplied the Europeans with an abundant work-force, and the slave trade became established. To work in their American colonies, the Portuguese, English and French needed slaves. They set up a "triangular trade" linking Europe, West Africa (where the slaves were captured) and America (where they were sold). From the 16th to the 19th centuries, more than eleven million Africans were deported to America, packed in slave ships in unhealthy conditions and maltreated. Around 10 to 15 percent of this human cargo died before arriving in America. In southern Africa, the Dutch founded a colony at Cape Town, not far from the Cape of Good Hope. This settlement was an important staging-post on the sea route to India and Indonesia. Later, the British occupied it and expanded the colonization of southern Africa.

Oceania

Oceania is made up of the islands of the Pacific Ocean, the largest of which is Australia. The peoples of the Pacific lived from fishing, growing crops and keeping livestock. For a long time, this area of the globe remained the least known in Europe, but after the first discoveries of the 16th century, exploration was carried out scientifically. Geographers sought to prove the existence of an "austral" continent, one located in the southern hemisphere. "Australia" is the name given to the immense territory finally discovered. In 1766-1769, the French navigator Bougainville sailed around the world and in the Pacific Ocean discovered the Polynesian islands, among the largest of which is Tahiti. The account of his voyage described these islands as a paradise on earth. From 1768, the British sailor Captain James Cook led three expeditions to every corner of the Pacific, from Hawaii to New Zealand. He explored the coasts of Australia, claiming these lands on behalf of Britain, established an exact map of Oceania and sailed as far south as the Antarctic circle. □

African statue of a Portuguese soldier, made between the 16th and 17th ◄ centuries in the kingdom of Benin.

The royal art of Benin

In the 16th and 17th centuries, before the slave trade decimated the population, the kings of Benin gave protection to artists who worked copper, gold, wood and ivory.

Such artists were in the exclusive service of the kings. They carved real subjects, such as the Portuguese soldiers who at the beginning of the 16th century landed in Africa equipped with steel helmets and swords. They also sculpted the heads of their kings, but here the purpose was religious. The heads, such as that above, have a flat base plate for placing on altars. Only the kings of Benin and the queen mothers were represented in this way. At the end of the 16th century, the importation of bronze by the Portuguese brought significant changes to the art of Benin.

the indu

al age

Technological discoveries in the 19th century led to the growth of industry and upheavals in society. Nationalist movements changed the frontiers of traditional states.

Europe

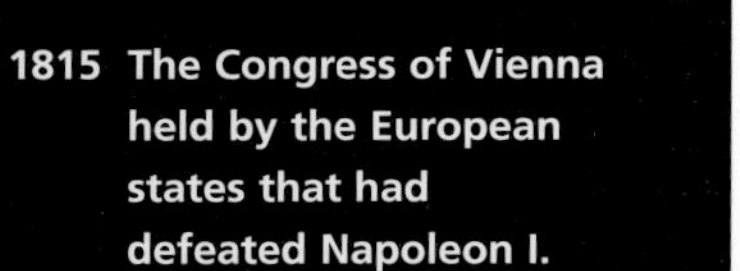

1815 The Congress of Vienna held by the European states that had defeated Napoleon I.
1824 Britain recognizes the right of workers to form trade unions.
1830 Revolts in Warsaw (Poland) and in France. Independence of Greece.
1830 Creation of Belgium.
1834 First electric motor.
1837-1901 Victoria, queen of England.
1840s First industrial crisis.
1848 Revolutions in most of the countries of Europe.
1848-1916 Franz Josef, emperor of Austria.
1852-1870 Napoleon III, emperor of the French.
1859-1861 War of Italian states for independence from Austria.
1861 Proclamation of the kingdom of Italy.
1861 Russia: Tsar Alexander II abolishes serfdom.
1866 War between Prussia and Austria, which is excluded from the German Confederation.
1870-1871 War between France and Prussia. French defeat. Proclamation of the German Empire.
1895 First public film screening.

In the 19th century, Europe underwent an industrial revolution. European countries, which were mainly agricultural at the beginning of the century, gradually came to be dominated by industry and commerce. This "industrialization" was accompanied by a transformation of society.
The period is also characterized by a rise in nationalism. From Spain to Poland, from Scandinavia to Sicily, the spread of new ideas called into question the role of the Church, of the aristocracy and of monarchs.

A steam locomotive in 1830. ▼

Technological advances

Scientific discoveries and technological advances that began in the 18th century expanded in the 19th century and gradually spread all over Europe. They led to what is known as the industrial revolution, which began in Britain around 1800 and then took hold in France, Germany, Switzerland and Belgium, and later in Russia. Industry made it possible to manufacture items in great numbers. It made use of new sources of energy, such as steam and electricity, and new technological processes. Inventions followed in quick succession: in 1834, the first electric motor was made; in 1876, communication by telephone became possible; 1885 was the year of the first antirabies vaccine and the first motor vehicle; 1895 saw the first film screening; 1903 the first powered flight. At this time, technological progress was seen as the key to improving living conditions.

New social classes

In the 19th century, landowners became less important. Prosperity no longer derived mainly from land but from industry and commerce, through which some families rapidly became rich. These families owned the factories and the machines—the "means of production"—and lived in the towns and cities. They formed a new social class: the wealthy industrialists. At the same period, country people were drawn to the cities, where there was a growing need for factory workers. On the land, machines were increasingly used in place of farmworkers. Another social class emerged: those employed in the factories, the workers. In the 1840s,

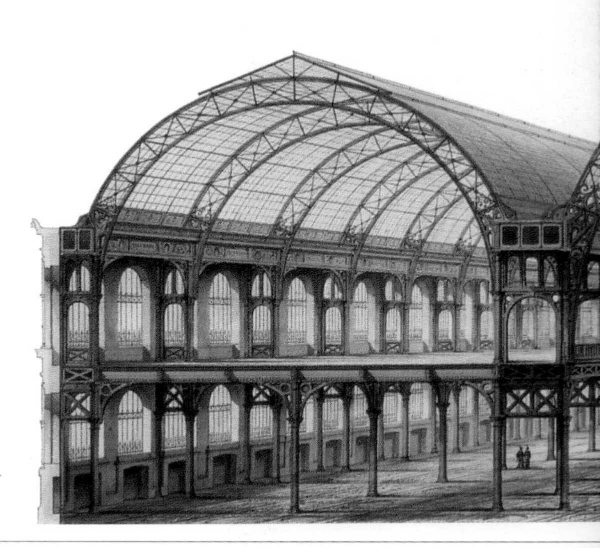

Workers demonstrate in Italy.

industrial expansion was checked by one of its first crises. Unemployment grew, and workers packed into the towns had no means to live. In order to defend their interests and rights, workers came together to form trade unions. Governments suspected that these organizations would encourage revolution and tried to prevent their formation. However, trade unions gradually acquired the legal right to exist. The first trade unions—the name indicates that the union brought together workers of the same trade—appeared in 1824 in Britain. In France, Germany and Austria unions were not permitted until the end of the century.

The development of ideas

In every sphere, including art, ideas clashed. Those who regretted the disappearance of the old order often expressed "world weariness" in romantic literature. Others believed in science and the material progress of humanity. Writers and philosophers who reflected on the organization of society included the French authors Victor Hugo and Emile Zola, who wrote about the problems caused by the changes in society. Charles Dickens did the same in Britain, as did Maxim Gorki in Russia and the Germans Karl Marx and Friedrich Engels. The transformation of society inspired philosophies that were often revolutionary. Socialism, for example, proposed a new organization of society and a government based on equality for all people. □

Karl Marx (1818-1883) ▲

For the German philosopher Karl Marx, history was marked by the class struggle between those people who own property and factories (the means of production) and those who produce. This theory is called Marxism.

P. J. Proudhon (1809-1865)

For the French socialist P. J. Proudhon, the ideal society was one in which production was so well-organized that the state would become useless. His ideas were among those at the root of anarchism. ▼

In the 19th century, the use of iron and steel frames for construction developed. This is a sketch for the Gare d'Orsay in Paris. ▼

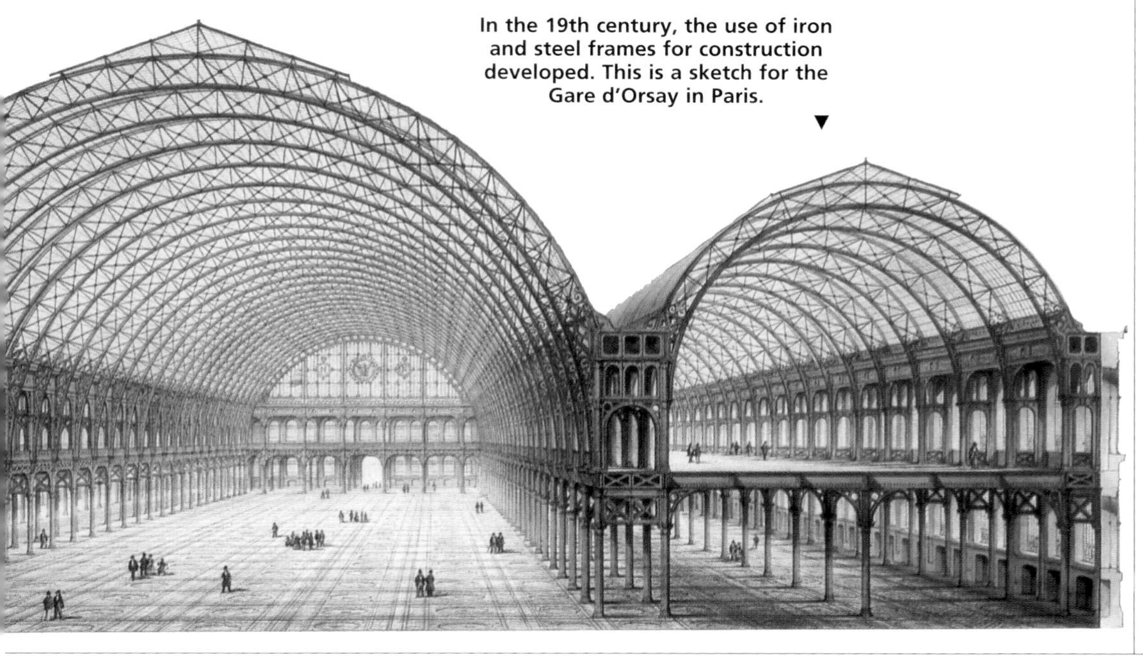

Coronation in 1837 of Queen Victoria of Great Britain.

The Europe of nations

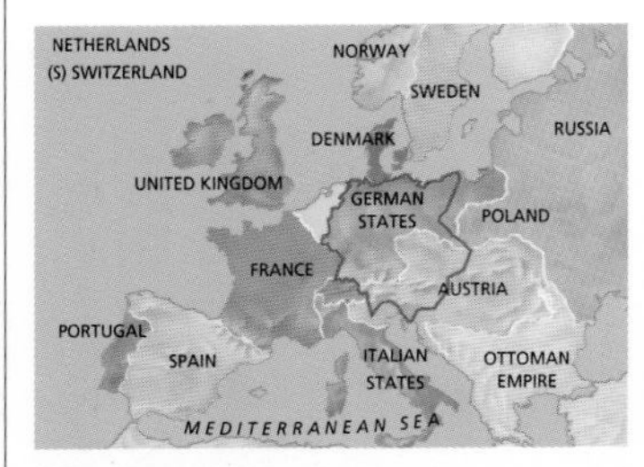

—— German Confederation

Europe in 1815 ▲

Some of the states with frontiers defined by the Congress of Vienna were made up of different nationalities: examples are Austria, the Ottoman Empire and Russia.

Belgium, a young nation

Beginning in 1815, the Catholic and partly French-speaking nation of Belgium was part of the kingdom of Holland. In 1830, the Belgians revolted and the great European powers finally recognized the new state and its new king, Leopold I. ▼

The emperor Franz Josef of Austria and his officers, about 1863.

At the end of the Napoleonic wars in 1815, the European powers (Britain, Austria, Prussia and Russia) met in Vienna to establish a lasting peace. They signed the Holy Alliance under which they swore to give assistance to each other whenever necessary. France, which was again ruled by a king, Louis XVIII, joined this alliance in 1818. However, the treaty did not take into account the popular will in many parts of Europe, and before long revolutions broke out across the continent.

Europe of the monarchies

In 1830, after a short revolution that brought down Charles X, France became a constitutional monarchy. While a new king,

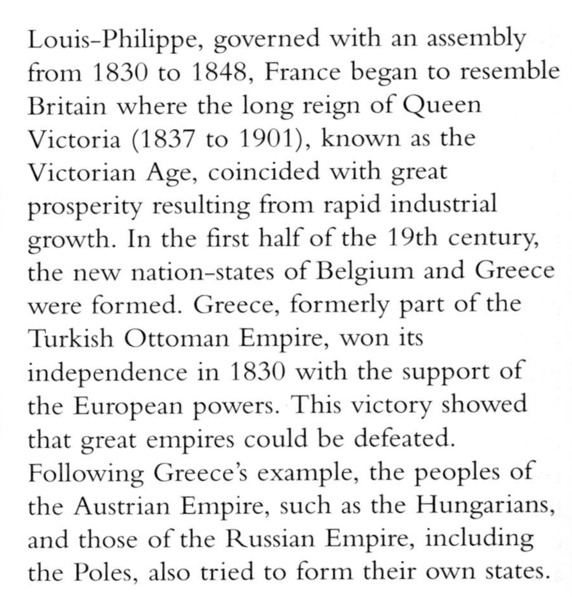

Louis-Philippe, governed with an assembly from 1830 to 1848, France began to resemble Britain where the long reign of Queen Victoria (1837 to 1901), known as the Victorian Age, coincided with great prosperity resulting from rapid industrial growth. In the first half of the 19th century, the new nation-states of Belgium and Greece were formed. Greece, formerly part of the Turkish Ottoman Empire, won its independence in 1830 with the support of the European powers. This victory showed that great empires could be defeated. Following Greece's example, the peoples of the Austrian Empire, such as the Hungarians, and those of the Russian Empire, including the Poles, also tried to form their own states.

Revolutionaries of 1848 ▶ on a barricade in Vienna, Austria.

The king of Prussia, Wilhelm I, was declared Kaiser of Germany in 1871.

1848: Europe of the revolutions

In 1848, revolutions broke out in many European states. These movements were linked to the economic problems of the 1840s and also to awakening national consciousness in various countries. The revolutionaries were in many cases socialists, and they demanded justice and freedom. The first revolt was in Paris, where the people rose up against King Louis-Philippe and proclaimed the Second Republic. Next Vienna, the capital of Austria, turned out the chancellor (the head of government), and a rising of the Czech and Hungarian peoples followed. The peoples of the German confederation of 39 states wanted to unite in a single nation. The Italians, whose country was divided into several kingdoms, also wanted to unite and free themselves from rule by Austria. This wave of insurrections was short-lived. In six to eight months, the revolutions were put down and the national movements crushed as government forces fought insurgents. The dead numbered in the thousands.

A new Europe

Despite the repression, important rights were won in Austria and in Russia, where Tsar Alexander II, who reigned from 1855, undertook such major reforms as the abolition of serfdom in 1861. He promoted the industrial development of Russia, which by then extended from the Black Sea to Siberia. In France, Napoleon III (nephew of Napoleon Bonaparte) proclaimed the Second Empire in 1852. In Italy, Victor Emmanuel II, king of Sardinia, and his minister Camillo Cavour, helped by Napoleon III, ousted the Austrians in 1859. This started the process of Italian unification, largely completed by Garibaldi. He led the Expedition of the Thousand (1,000 freedom fighters) to Sicily in 1860 and from there conquered southern Italy. The kingdom of Italy was proclaimed in 1861. The Prussian chancellor, Otto von Bismarck, took control of the movement for German unity. Prussia defeated Austria in 1866. Then, in 1870, Bismarck directed a war that brought all the German states together against France and was again victorious. The German empire, the Reich, which symbolized the unity of the country, was proclaimed on 18 January 1871 at Versailles, in defeated France. □

The Italian patriot Giuseppe Garibaldi during the Expedition of the Thousand. ►

Constitution of the Swiss state in 1848 ▲

From the Middle Ages, Switzerland had been organized in a confederation of states known as the cantons, each of which enjoyed a degree of autonomy. In 1848, these cantons gave themselves a new constitution, establishing a system that has lasted up to the present day. A neutral country, Switzerland was a refuge for fleeing revolutionaries including French, Italians, Hungarians, Poles and Russians. Based on the same principle of neutrality, Switzerland became the base for such institutions as the Red Cross, founded by Henri Dunant in 1859. The Swiss city of Geneva became an important center for diplomatic negotiations. It was there in 1864 that the European states signed the convention on the rights of wounded and captured soldiers.

After three centuries of colonization, Latin America won its independence. In the United States, the conquest of the West marked the beginning of unprecedented economic growth on the continent.

The Americas

1816 José de San Martín declares the independence of Argentina.
1821 Mexico becomes independent.
1822 Brazil becomes an independent empire.
1849 California gold rush.
1859 United States: first oil wells in Pennsylvania.
1860 Abraham Lincoln elected president of the United States.
1861-1865 United States: Civil war between the northern and southern states ends in victory for the North.
1861-1890 Indian wars: the Cheyenne, the Dakota and later the Apache resist the advance of the settlers.
1867 Canada obtains autonomy from Great Britain.
1867 Mexico: Benito Juárez has the Archduke of Austria, Maximilian, shot.
1869 United States: construction of the first transcontinental railway linking the East of the country to the West.
1886 United States: strikes in Chicago are violently put down.
1911 Mexico: revolution against the authoritarian government of Porfirio Díaz.

In the 19th century, the countries of Latin America (Central America and South America) followed the example of their northern neighbor, the United States, and gradually achieved independence. In the United States itself, people began to move from areas settled since the early 1600s century into the West.

The revolutions in Latin America

A large part of South America formerly under Spanish rule was independent by 1830. In Argentina, José de San Martín led the liberation movement and proclaimed the country's independence in 1816. He also liberated Chile in 1818 and Peru in 1821. General Simon Bolívar won independence for Venezuela in 1811 and for Colombia in 1819. Although new states had been formed, the authoritarian regimes that were set up undertook no real reforms and revolutions continued to occur. Brazil was an exception.

General Simon Bolívar in 1821.

The conquest of the North American West.

This former Portuguese colony became an independent empire in 1822, governed by the Portuguese prince Pedro I. The country then underwent marked economic growth. In 1889, the emperor was overthrown by the army, which took power. Mexico, which became independent in 1821, was governed from 1824 to 1855 by the authoritarian Santa Anna. In 1858, Benito Juárez led a revolutionary movement and became president of the republic in 1861. He opposed the Hapsburg Archduke Maximilian of Austria, who with French help proclaimed himself emperor of Mexico in 1864, and had him executed in 1867. In 1876, General Porfirio Díaz seized power and reestablished peace, and Mexico enjoyed a period of high economic growth. However, social inequalities multiplied and caused popular revolts. These culminated in 1911, in a revolution led by Pancho Villa and Emiliano Zapata.

The battle of Shiloh, Tennessee, in 1862 during the American Civil War.

The conquest of the West

The United States, formed by a federation of states, expanded in the 19th century to include the new states of Louisiana, Florida, Oregon and Texas, among others. Until 1850, the country was divided into three areas: the Northeast, the South and the Pacific Coast. In the center were vast tracts that remained Indian lands. However, European immigrants (nearly 5 million came to the United States between 1830 and 1860 and 20 million between 1860 and 1914) took new lands from the Indian tribes in what was to be the conquest of the West. The Indian peoples rose up against the advance of the American settlers, notably the Dakota and their chief Sitting Bull. The Indians were defeated; many were massacred and others were sent to live on reservations.

Following the election of Abraham Lincoln to the presidency of the United States in 1860, the northern states dominated the Union. Lincoln wanted to end slavery in the southern states, which decided to leave the Union. They formed the Confederacy and seceded. This decision led to the Civil War between the northern and southern states that lasted from 1861 to 1865. It ended with victory for the north, which abolished slavery. Woodrow Wilson won the presidential elections of 1912 and guided his country towards a closer relationship with Europe.

Industrial America

New York, Chicago and Detroit became large industrial cities. The American success story was that of men such as John D. Rockefeller who—often starting out with nothing—built huge financial empires based on coal, steel, railways or oil. This rapid growth was achieved at the expense of the workers, who had few industrial rights. They organized major strikes, such as the 1886 Chicago strike, which was violently put down. Eventually, forming trade unions was authorized and the government passed laws to restrict the influence of powerful financial groupings. □

◄ President Abraham Lincoln of the United States supported the abolition of slavery.

The United States

The Civil War between the states lasted from 1861 to 1865.

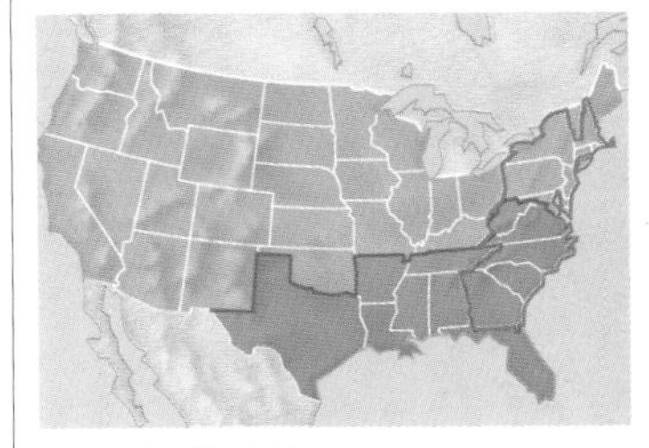

The first 13 states

Confederacy of the southern states

Union of the northern states

Canada

France ceded Canada to Britain by the Treaty of Paris in 1763. The French Canadians struggled to maintain a distinctive French culture, the French language, their Catholic religion and political representation. In 1867, Canada was given a constitution and became the Canadian Confederation. Below, the Chateau de Frontenac in the French-speaking city of Quebec. ▼

From 1867, Japan began to make its mark as a great world power. The Chinese empire and India were dominated by foreign powers, while the Ottoman Empire collapsed.

Asia: Japan and

- **1818** India: the British defeat the Marathas and strengthen their control over the country.
- **1839-1861** Ottoman Empire: the sultan Abdülmecid institutes reforms.
- **1839-1842** China: Opium War won by Britain. "Unequal" treaties between China and the European states. Hong Kong is ceded to Britain.
- **1857-1858** India: the Mutiny or Great Rebellion. End of the Mogul Empire.
- **1867-1912** Japan: reign of emperor Mutsuhito. The Meiji era.
- **1876** Queen Victoria becomes Empress of India.
- **1885** Founding of the Congress Party in India.
- **1894-1895** War between China and Japan.
- **1900** China: the Boxer rebellion.
- **1905** War between Russia and Japan. Victory for Japan.
- **1909** Turkey: the Young Turks movement takes power.
- **1911** China: end of the Manchu Empire and proclamation of the Republic.
- **1912** China: Sun Yat-sen founds the Nationalist People's Party.

In the 19th century, Japan opened up to Western influences and confirmed its power. At the same period, China found it difficult to resist European incursions into its territory as imperial power weakened. The Mogul Empire of India was taken over by Britain. The Ottoman Empire, which governed various peoples, was gradually broken up into smaller territories.

Japan, a great power

In the 19th century, Japan was governed by the emperor, who lived in the old capital of Kyoto, and the shogun, the military chief, who wielded real power from the new city of Edo. The country was in crisis and the peasants lived in poverty. In 1854 the shogun was obliged to sign a trade agreement with the American admiral Perry and then agreements with the British, Russians and Dutch. From this point, Westerners were allowed to move into Japan. In 1867, a new emperor, Mutsuhito, came to the throne and set his country on the path to industrial revolution. Taking the Western countries as a model, he suppressed the military government of the shogun, gave his country a constitution and set up a Parliament. The imperial capital was transferred from Kyoto to Edo, which was renamed Tokyo. A new period began: the Meiji era, which means "enlightened government." Transformation was rapid as towns, roads, factories and transport systems developed. Japan became an

A 1906 street scene in China shows two porters and a Buddhist monk.

Arrival of American troops in Yokohama, Japan, in 1854.

China

industrial and military power. Mutsuhito took the island of Formosa (Taiwan) from the Chinese in 1895. Intending then to extend his domination to Korea, he found himself opposed by Russia, which had in 1860 established a base in the Siberian city of Vladivostok, close to Korea. This rivalry led to war between Russia and Japan in 1904, ending in Japanese victory in 1905.

A weakened China

In the 19th century, China gradually lost the power it had held in the previous century as the Manchu emperor's influence waned. The country's internal situation worsened: taxes rose, and the population grew and got poorer. The imperial administration was disorganized. Europeans wanted to develop trade, but China remained closed. In 1839, the Opium War, so called because it was fought over the opium trade, broke out between the Chinese authorities and the British. Several "unequal" treaties, unfavorable for the Chinese, were signed in 1844 and 1860. These gave Westerners concessions in China, territories that were not subject to Chinese laws. The zones of foreign influence widened: in the north, the Russians; in the east, the Japanese, Germans and Americans; in the south, the French; in the southwest and in Shanghai and Hong Kong, the British.

The Chinese Republic replaces the Manchu Empire

Nationalist movements opposed the Western presence in China and the policy of the imperial government. Revolts broke out, including the nationalist revolt of the secret society of the Boxers in 1900. Empress Cixi (Tz'u-hsi) and the Chinese government

Tramway in the streets of Tokyo, Japan, in 1905.

appealed for foreign troops to restore order. The revolts were repressed but the determination to make China an independent nation was reinforced. In 1905, the reformist politician Sun Yat-sen founded a movement which in 1912 became the Nationalist People's Party (Guomindang); his intention was to make China a republic. In 1911, the last emperor, Puyi, was forced to abdicate. A republic was proclaimed at Nanjing, but Sun Yat-sen did not have the power he needed. The new regime had to confront warlords who imposed their own law in the regions of China which they controlled. In 1911 and 1912, the Chinese provinces of Mongolia and Tibet declared their independence. In Manchuria, a province with a Chinese population, Japanese influence became dominant. □

Sun Yat-sen and his wife

In 1894 Sun Yat-sen created the Association for the Revival of China. In 1905, he founded a movement with the aims of "independence, democracy, welfare." This was the basis of the Guomindang, the political party he created in 1912. Elected president of the Republic in 1911, Sun Yat-sen later had to flee from general Yuan Shih-kai. He returned to China in 1917, was reelected in 1921 and formed an alliance with the communist party led by Mao Zedong. On his death in 1925, he was succeeded by his wife's brother, Chiang Kai-shek. ▼

An Indian maharajah receives important visitors to his kingdom during the 18th century.

India and the Middle East

Prince Ardshir Mirza

This prince ruled Teheran, capital of the empire of Iran. Iran was a Muslim state, governed by a sovereign known as the Shah. In the 19th century, the Shah was forced to deal with the arrival of Europeans—the Russians and British who wanted to extend their influence in the Middle East by establishing

themselves in Iran. Between 1813 and 1828, the Russians conquered territories near the Caspian Sea (modern Georgia and Azerbaijan) which had been Iranian. The Iranians resisted, but in 1907 the British and Russians signed an agreement by which Iran was split into three zones: the northwest under Russian influence, the southeast under British influence and the center, which was to remain neutral.

East Indians revolting against the British. (Malakhan, 1897).

At the beginning of the 19th century, India was ruled by the Mogul emperors, and the Ottoman Empire dominated almost all of the Middle East. However, the industrial revolution, the European intrusion and nationalist movements were to bring about major changes.

The end of the Mogul Empire

At the beginning of the 19th century in India, the Mogul emperor tolerated the trading activities of the East India Company and the presence of the British. To extend their influence, the British fought against several Indian states, including the Maratha confederation formed of independent states in the northwest of India. The Marathas were defeated in 1818. From this point, the British were firmly established in India. They introduced the telegraph and the railway and developed cotton, jute and tea plantations. Christian missionaries came to India. Some Indian rulers accepted the new order, but many Indians objected to the British

Maharajahs on a tiger hunt in India. ▼

Mural in Rajasthan showing the arrival of the railway in India.

presence. Resistance flared in 1857 when sepoys, Indian soldiers (both Muslim and Hindu) under the command of British officers, rose in rebellion, which the British called the Indian Mutiny. The Mogul Emperor Bahadur II supported the rebels. The British put down the uprising and deprived the Mogul emperor of his powers. In 1858, India became a full British colony.

British India

British India included territories directly administered by Britain and others governed by Indian princes, the maharajahs. Britain's Queen Victoria became Empress of India in 1876. Her representative was a viceroy who governed the country first from the city of Calcutta and after 1912 from Delhi, the old Mogul capital. Important Indian families adapted to the European way of life while retaining their own culture. At the same time, Indian nationalist movements formed, and in 1885 the Congress Party, which wanted India represented in the British parliament, was founded. Voting rights under certain conditions were granted to Indian representatives. In 1906, the Muslims, traditional opponents of the Hindus, formed their own Muslim League. As they made up the majority population in the Indus valley and the Ganges delta, the Muslims campaigned for substantial political rights.

The breakup of the Ottoman Empire

In the 19th century, the Ottoman Turks gradually lost control of a number of provinces in their empire. In 1830, sultan Mahmoud II had to recognize the independence of Greece and the conquest of Algeria by France. His successor embarked on a policy of reforms. However, in 1876, after the Crimean War fought by Russia against France, Britain and the Ottoman Empire, the Turks became dominated by their powerful allies. The country was hugely in debt and depended on the aid of the Europeans, who intervened in its internal affairs. From 1876 to 1909 during the reign of Sultan Abdülhamid II, all reforms were blocked. In the Arabian peninsula, the Turks tried to restore their old authority over the Arabs without success. Supporters of reform then joined in the Young Turks movement which opposed the arbitrary power of the sultan and the presence of foreigners. Officers including Mustapha Kemal and Enver Pasha secretly supported this movement, which took power in 1909. Enver Pasha was appointed minister of war in 1914 and brought the Ottoman Empire into the First World War on Germany's side. After its defeat, the empire was finally dismantled at the end of the war. □

A family of distinguished Vietnamese ▲

The empire of Vietnam, founded by the Nguyen dynasty at the beginning of the 19th century, dominated the peninsula of Indochina. This area close to China had a valuable natural resource: rubber, made from latex obtained from the sap of the rubber tree. Indochina was conquered and colonized from 1883 by France, which seized the kingdoms of Laos and Cambodia as well as Vietnam. The colonial authorities set up a protectorate, a system that controlled the existing administration in each country. The Vietnamese did not give up their independence easily. They staged several revolts that were harshly repressed by France.

Enver Pasha, commander-in-chief of the Turkish armies. ▼

In the 19th century, Africa was colonized by foreign powers. By molding new countries in their own images, the colonial powers often shattered traditional African cultures.

Africa

1804 Founding of the Sokoto empire (Niger-Nigeria).
1805-1848 Egypt: reign of Mehemet Ali.
1830 The French take Algiers.
1832 Abd-el-Kader resists the French in Algeria.
1834-1839 The Boers found Natal, Transvaal and the Orange Free State.
1847 Founding of Liberia.
1869 Egypt: opening of the Suez Canal.
1885 Conference of Berlin.
1883-1898 Sudan rebellion, put down by the British.
1899-1902 South Africa: the Boer War.
1910 Constitution of the Union of South Africa.
1912 Union of South Africa: creation of the African National Congress (ANC).

French colonists and Arabs at an Algerian oasis.

In the 19th century, North Africa freed itself from the Ottoman Turks, only to face a gradual takeover by Europeans. Muslim empires were founded in black Africa, where European expansion also continued. By the end of the century, almost all of Africa was colonized by European states.

In North Africa

In the 19th century, Egypt was freed by the Pasha (viceroy) Mehemet Ali from the domination of the Ottoman Turks. The Egyptian rulers wanted to modernize their country, and they appealed to Europeans for help with major works. As a result, the Suez Canal, through which ships pass from the Mediterranean to the Red Sea, was built between 1859 and 1869 under the direction of the French engineer, Ferdinand de Lesseps. This policy was very costly and Egyptians got into debt. They accepted that Europeans should run the administration. The British extended their domination over Egypt, which in 1914 became a British protectorate (a protectorate is a country under the control of another country). Sudan, conquered by Egypt between 1820 and 1840, rebelled in 1883. Mohammed Ahmed, known as the Mahdi, created an independent Muslim state in the Sudan. The British, led by Lord Kitchener, put down the rebellion in 1898, and the Sudan became a British-Egyptian possession. The countries of the Maghreb also fell under European control. In 1830, French troops took Algiers. Although the

◄ A horseman and foot soldier of the Ashanti people of Ghana, about 1840.

Capture of the camp of Abd el-Kader by the French in Algeria, 1843.

emir (Arab prince) Abd el-Kader tried to resist French occupation, he was finally forced to surrender in 1847. French settlement in Algeria marked the beginning of its colonization. Tunisia in 1881 and then Morocco in 1912 also became French protectorates. Libya came under Italian control in 1912.

Colonization in black Africa

New kingdoms were founded in black Africa in the 19th century. In 1804, the Peul people, led by Ousmane dan Fodio, founded the Sokoto Empire in present-day Niger and Nigeria. In 1854, El Hadj Omar founded a Muslim state that included modern Senegal and Mali and was maintained by his son until 1900. In central Africa, the ruler Rabah extended his power south of Lake Chad. In 1847, the state of Liberia on the Atlantic coast was founded for freed black slaves from the United States. The constitution of this republic was drafted on the U.S. model. European exploration in black Africa increased. Missionaries spread the Christian religion as colonists and companies moved in. In 1884 and 1885, a conference of the European powers in Berlin defined their respective spheres of influence. The Portuguese retained Angola and Mozambique; France, a large part of West Africa; Britain, eastern and southern Africa. In central Africa, the king of the Belgians took the Congo (formerly Zaire).

City of Segou in Mali, 1901. ▲

In South Africa

The colony founded at the Cape by the Dutch became British in 1814. The Boers, colonists of Dutch origin, did not accept British rule. They migrated inland in what is known as the Great Trek, set up new states and worked the gold mines discovered in the area around Johannesburg. Mining companies brought in new immigrants. The Boers again felt threatened by the British, and this led to the Boer War (1899-1902), which ended with victory for Britain. In 1910, the Union of South Africa was set up, bringing together several states. Blacks—65 percent of the population—had no share of power and were gradually relegated to "homelands." The African National Congress (ANC) was founded in 1912 to fight for black African rights and later campaigned against South Africa's policy of apartheid (racial separation). □

◄ Zulu warrior of Southern Africa.

Stanley and Livingstone

In 1870, the U.S. journalist Henry Morton Stanley set out for Africa in search of the British explorer Dr. David Livingstone, who was presumed missing. He found the doctor in 1871 on the shores of Lake Tanganyika. Livingstone, a missionary, was one of the first and greatest white explorers of Africa. Stanley too became famous and explored along the Congo River. In 1879 he offered his services to the king of the Belgians, Leopold II. He founded Stanleyville (modern Kisangani) in the Congo. ▼

Rivalries between European countries at the end of the 19th century led to the outbreak of the First World War in August 1914, which caused millions of deaths and profound changes to the contemporary world.

The First World War

1882 Alliance between Germany, Austria-Hungary and Italy: the Triple Alliance.
1907 Alliance between Russia, Britain and France: the Triple Entente.
1914 June: assassination of the heir to Austria-Hungary in Sarajevo. August: start of the First World War.
1915 Trench warfare on the Western Front. Eastern Front: advance of the Austrians and Germans against the Russians. Italy joins the allied side (Triple Entente).
1916 Western Front: battle of Verdun. Eastern Front: retreat of the Russians.
1917 Revolution in Russia. End of the war on the Eastern Front. The United States joins the war on the side of Britain and France.
1918 January: U.S. President Wilson tries to organize the peace terms. 11 November: Armistice signed.
1919 28 June: Treaty of Versailles between the allies and Germany.
1919-1920 Peace treaties between the various countries that took part in the war.

After its victory over France in 1870, the German Empire became one of the most powerful countries in Europe. The other European states sought to contain this new force and at the end of the 19th century signed alliances against it. Two camps formed: in 1882, Germany, Austria-Hungary and Italy (which changed sides in 1915) formed the Triple Alliance. France allied with Russia in 1894 and then with Britain in 1904. From 1907, these three countries were joined in the Triple Entente.

The origins of the conflict

Both Russia and Austria-Hungary were weakened by internal problems but were attempting to extend their control over the Balkans (Bulgaria, Serbia, Bosnia-Herzegovina). Other claims complicated the situation. The French wanted to reconquer the territories of Alsace and Lorraine, which had been in the German Empire since 1870. The kingdom of Italy wanted to take over Italian-populated areas still under Austrian control (the cities of Fiume and Trieste, and the regions of Trentino and Dalmatia). Several European countries were also involved in colonial wars, especially in Africa. From 1910, all the countries prepared for a conflict that seemed impossible to avoid. Germany and Russia reinforced their armies. In 1913, France increased the length of military service to three years. War finally broke out after the assassination of Archduke Franz Ferdinand, heir of Austria-Hungary, in Sarajevo, Bosnia, on 28 June 1914. By August 1914, the conflict had spread to all the countries of the Triple Alliance and the Triple Entente.

The confrontation

The war rapidly unfolded on two fronts: the Western Front, where the Germans invaded Belgium and the north of France in August 1914, and the Eastern Front, where the German armies faced the Russians. After the

Life for soldiers in the trenches.

Soldiers attack with bayonets in 1916.

Airplanes were used during the 1914-1918 war. ▲

first battles during the winter of 1914, the Western Front became static. Soldiers dug trenches and were ordered not to retreat. There they lived in appalling conditions: in dirt and mud, badly fed and on edge waiting for the next attack. Trench warfare introduced the use of new weapons, including poison gas. The terrible battle of Verdun, in the east of France, lasted ten months in 1916 and caused tens of thousands of deaths without either the French or Germans changing their original positions. The war became worldwide as overseas colonies took part: Africans, Indians and Australians fought alongside the Europeans, and battles took place in Africa, the Middle East and Asia. In 1917, after three years of war, the adversaries were weakened. Russia, where revolution had overthrown the tsar, withdrew from the war, and its representatives signed an armistice with the Germans. The Eastern Front ceased to exist and the Germans could concentrate their efforts on the Western Front. In the same year, the United States entered the war on the side of Britain and France. On 18 January 1918, the U.S. president Woodrow Wilson set out 14 conditions for the establishment of a lasting peace. Germany signed the armistice, ending the war, on 11 November 1918 at Rethondes in France.

Victors and vanquished

The emperors of Germany and Austria-Hungary abdicated in 1918, and peace treaties were signed in France in 1919 and 1920. The Treaty of Versailles imposed on Germany by the allies in June 1919 was very harsh. Germany's frontiers were changed and its colonies taken away. It was no longer allowed an army. Considered responsible for the war, it was to pay the allies 269 billion gold marks as damages. Other treaties decided the fate of the countries making up the Austro-Hungarian Empire, which was dissolved. Austria became a republic, and new states were created in central Europe. The Ottoman Empire was broken up. The First World War caused 8 million deaths, destroyed a generation and laid waste entire regions. □

Europe in 1914

The countries were divided into two camps, the Triple Alliance and the Triple Entente.

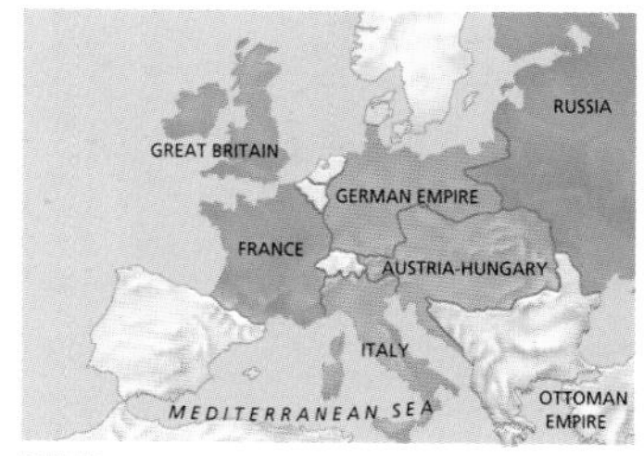

Triple Alliance
Triple Entente

British soldiers loading a machine gun

Invented at the end of the 19th century, the machine gun was one of the most deadly weapons of the First World War. Other new weapons were perfected, among them howitzers, poison gas and tanks. Airplanes fought duels and made it possible to carry out reconnaissance behind enemy lines. ▼

the contem

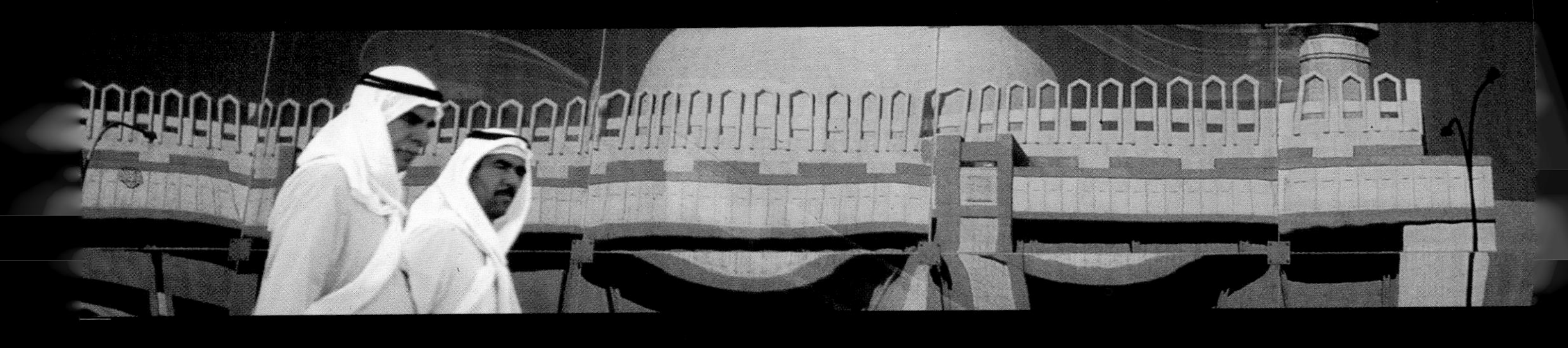

rary world

The 1917 revolution ended the Russian Empire. Lenin took power as leader of the communists. The new state, the Union of Soviet Socialist Republics, was created in 1922. Stalin succeeded Lenin.

From Russia to the USSR

1917 February: first phase of the revolution. March: abdication of the tsar. October: second phase of the revolution; the soviets take power. December: Lenin signs an armistice with Germany.
918 Assassination of the imperial family. Civil war between the supporters of the tsar and the Bolsheviks, until 1920. Creation of the Red Army.
919 March: foundation of the Third Communist International.
922 December: official constitution of the USSR.
924 January: death of Lenin.
929 Stalin launches the first Five-Year Plan.
930 Beginning of massive deportations to the work camps.
939 Nazi-Soviet non-aggression pact.

Bolshevik demonstration during the 1917 revolution.

The USSR emerged after the 1917 October revolution in the control of Lenin. He led the Bolshevik party, which applied the principles of socialism and communism, as defined by Marx (see p. 73). After Lenin, the USSR came under Stalin's rule.

The 1917 revolution

At the beginning of the 20th century, Russia was governed by Tsar Nicholas II, who wielded absolute power. Peasants made up 85 percent of the population, but in the cities, workers were increasing in numbers. Their often poor living conditions grew worse during the First World War, which began in 1914. Serious rioting broke out in February 1917, accompanied by widespread strikes and demonstrations. Nicholas II was forced to abdicate on 15 March. This was the first stage of the revolution. A provisional government was set up. In major cities such as Moscow and St. Petersburg, soviets—councils (or committees) of workers and soldiers—formed. The communist Bolsheviks were very influential in these. In October 1917, the second stage of the revolution started. The Bolsheviks seized power, with Lenin at their head. Lenin formed a new government and applied a strict program: suppression of large land holdings and land distribution to the peasants; establishment of worker control in the factories. In December, Lenin signed an armistice with Germany so that Russia was no longer at war. In 1918, the imperial family was assassinated. A civil war broke out between the Whites,

Lenin addressing factory workers in 1917.

supporters of the tsar, and the Reds, the communists. It ended in 1920 with communist victory. Two years later, the USSR (the Union of Soviet Socialist Republics) was created.

The Communist International

In 1918, the revolutionary ideas of the Bolsheviks took hold in Germany and Hungary, where soviets attempted to take power. There were disturbances in many countries, even as far afield as China, but governments put down the uprisings. In 1919, the Third International, an international association of workers, was founded in Moscow. It associated with Soviet Russia most of the revolutionary parties sharing the common goal of taking action to transform society. The European socialist parties, which had existed since the 19th century, were invited to join. They then divided between those who decided to join, the communists, and those who refused and kept the name of "socialists."

Stalin

After Lenin's death, Stalin gradually took control in the USSR and after 1927 set up a repressive authoritarian regime. Property became collective. From 1932, almost all lands were farmed as communes, as kolkhozes (peasant cooperatives) or sovkhozes (state farms). Production was organized in five-year plans that promoted heavy industry and vast building projects. By 1940, the Soviet Union had become one of the major industrial powers. From 1930 to his death in 1953, Stalin had millions of people deported to work in camps known as gulags, accused of opposing the revolution or the Soviet state. In 1939, isolated from the French and British democracies and confronted by the German threat, Stalin signed a non-aggression pact with Hitler. However, in 1941, during the Second World War, the USSR was invaded by Germany. □

Trotsky (1879-1940) ▲

A revolutionary colleague of Lenin, Trotsky became head of the Red Army. Seeing him as a rival successsor to Lenin, Stalin drove him from power and in 1927 had him expelled from the Communist Party. In 1929, Trotsky was deported and later expelled from the USSR. He was assassinated in Mexico in 1940.

Grigori Zinoviev (1883-1936) ▲

Zinoviev, a colleague of Lenin, joined Trotsky in the opposition in 1925. In the show trials held by Stalin from 1935 to 1936 in Moscow, Zinoviev was one of many Bolsheviks tried and sentenced to death.

Meeting of farm workers in the Ukraine, 1929. ▼

After the 1914-1918 war, the United States became the leading world power. However, in 1929, it went through a serious economic depression that also affected the rest of the industrialized world.

America between

- **1919-1933** United States: Prohibition era.
- **1929** Stock exchange crash in New York. Beginning of the economic crisis.
- **1930** Brazil: beginning of Getulio Vargas's dictatorship. Argentina: military coup d'état.
- **1931** Canada: independence within the British Commonwealth.
- **1932** United States: Franklin D. Roosevelt is elected president. He launches the New Deal to take the country out of depression.
- **1938** Mexico: president Lázaro Cárdenas nationalizes the oil industry.

After the First World War, the United States experienced more than a decade of extraordinary growth. Then in 1929 came a serious economic crisis that put American prosperity at risk, disrupted society and spread to the rest of the American continent and to Europe. Its effects were still being felt when the Second World War broke out in 1939.

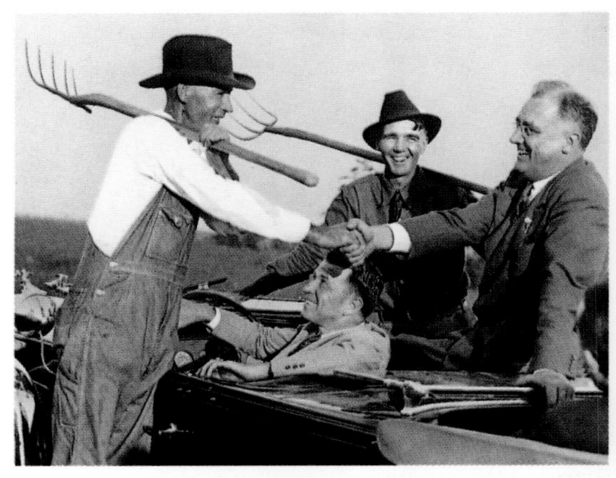

Franklin Roosevelt campaigning in Georgia before his election as president of the United States in 1932.

Prosperity in the United States

Two parties dominate U.S. politics: the conservative Republican party and the Democratic Party which favors less traditional economic and social policies. From 1919, the Republicans were in power. They isolated the country from the rest of the world, refusing to join the League of Nations, which had been set up in 1920 to guarantee peace. Believing in traditional values, they wanted to improve the morality of U.S. citizens; to this end, the Republicans sought to ban the manufacture, transport and sale of alcohol—a measure known as Prohibition. At the same time, the United States experienced extraordinary growth. This was the period of the Roaring Twenties, or the Jazz Age, as it was also known. Industrial production increased, in part due to new working methods invented by the "time-and-motion" engineer, Frederick W. Taylor. To save time and increase output, movements were simplified, tasks were timed and work was

Jazz musicians in the 1930s. ▼

Car factory in Detroit, USA, 1931.

the wars

done on a production line. Such methods made it possible to manufacture identical articles in quantity and so to sell more for less. Only very large companies had the resources to follow this practice. Examples were the Ford Motor Company, set up by Henry Ford, and General Motors, which at this time produced nearly two of every three American cars. In 1929, the United States was the world's leading economic power. Its banks lent money to the entire world, and the American standard of living was higher than anywhere else.

The 1929 crash

The Wall Street crash started on "Black Thursday," 24 October 1929. On that day, many shareholders, who no longer had any confidence in their companies, attempted to sell their shares. As a result, share prices plummeted. Many banks failed and the crisis soon spread throughout the U.S. economy. Industrial production fell, factories closed and the number of unemployed soared. It was the Great Depression. The crisis was one of the most important events of the interwar years. In 1930, it spread to Europe, first hitting Germany and Austria and then Britain and France. As they appeared incapable of solving the problems it brought, governments in many countries were questioned and undermined (see p. 92-99). In 1932, Americans elected the Democrat Franklin Delano Roosevelt as their president and, to overcome the crisis, he proposed a plan known as the New Deal. The federal government was to intervene in the economy, for example, by launching major public works. The New Deal was not completely successful in bringing the country out of crisis, but Roosevelt was reelected in 1936 and 1940.

Latin America

The 1929 depression had severe consequences in the countries of Latin America. In most of these countries, the economy depended on a single product—coffee in Brazil, copper in Chile, sugar in Cuba. During the depression, these products did not sell. Coffee surpluses were burned in Brazil, while two out of three miners were out of work in the copper mines of Chile. Such difficulties led to the seizure of power by military leaders. In Brazil, Getulio Vargas set up a dictatorship in 1930. In Argentina, the generals took power and the army kept control of the country until 1943. In Mexico, the revolution begun in 1911 (see p. 76) ended in 1920, after a long civil war. From this date, the military directed the country and began to industrialize it. Lázaro Cárdenas, who became president in 1934, nationalized the oil industry in 1938. In Chile, left-wing parties took power and President Aguirre Cerda set up a Chilean-style New Deal.

Cárdenas, president of Mexico from 1934 to 1940.

Prohibition (1919-1933) ▲

During Prohibition, drinking alcohol was illegal in the United States. This woman is hiding her liquor in her telephone.

Canada

Prime minister Mackenzie King (below) strengthened his country which, in 1931, became independent within the British Commonwealth. From this point, Canada recognized the British monarch as head of state but governed its own affairs. ▼

Between the two world wars, political upheavals took place across Europe. While the fascist party took power in Italy and the Nazis ruled in Germany, the democracies strove to preserve peace.

Europe: fascism

1919 Italy: founding of the fascist party by Mussolini. Germany: establishment of the republic.
1922 Italy: after the March on Rome, Mussolini becomes head of government.
1925 Italy: beginning of Mussolini's dictatorship.
1933 Germany: Hitler becomes chancellor.
1934 30 June, Germany: Night of the Long Knives.
1935 September, Germany: Nuremberg laws against the German Jews.
1936 Abdication crisis in Britain. In France, the Popular Front wins the elections. Spain: beginning of the civil war between Republicans and Fascists.
1938 September: at the Munich conference, Britain and France allow Hitler to annex part of Czechoslovakia.

Europe changed radically after the First World War. The old German and Austrian Empires no longer existed, and new states (Yugoslavia, Poland and Czechoslovakia) had been created in central Europe. In the 1920s, Europe gradually recovered from war, but the 1929 depression, which started in the United States, put an end to this growth. Governments that failed to solve the economic crisis were weakened, and in some countries, dictators seized power.

Fascism in Italy

In 1919, the kingdom of Italy was in crisis. Industry was in decline and unemployment increasing. Strikes broke out and workers occupied factories. The fascist party founded by Benito Mussolini seemed to many Italians the only force capable of reestablishing order. This political party was organized in disciplined groups, known as *fasci* in Italian. Its members, the Blackshirts, were mainly malcontents, major industrialists and landowners. In 1922, Mussolini called on the fascists to march on Rome, Italy's capital, and demand power. The king was forced to appoint him head of government, and from 1924, Mussolini set up a dictatorship, styling himself *duce* ("leader" in Italian). As head of the government and leader of the fascist party, Mussolini held all power. The fascist party controlled the press and radio, children were indoctrinated in youth movements and opponents were imprisoned or exiled to remote parts of the country. To demonstrate Italy's importance to the world, Mussolini launched ambitious public works and organized spectacular popular demonstrations.

Benito Mussolini greets the crowd gathered to acclaim him at Genoa, Italy, in 1938. ▼

Nazism in Germany

After the First World War, Germany became a republic. The country was practically ruined and experienced severe economic hardships which the government could not ease. Such conditions led to the growth of National Socialism and the Nazi party created by Adolf Hitler. In January 1933, Hitler became chancellor, or head of the German government, following the Nazis' victory in elections. He outlawed all other political parties and had leading party members who favored social reform assassinated, in what became known as the Night of the Long Knives. Hitler set up a dictatorship based on the Nazi party and forcibly applied the Nazi doctrine of extreme nationalism and theories of racial supremacy. In 1933, persecution of the Jews began (see p. 98). In 1935, the Nuremberg laws were passed against German Jews. In 1938, during the Night of the Broken Glass, many Jewish businesses were destroyed and 20,000 Jews were detained and sent to concentration

German soldiers at the Nuremberg rally in 1938.

and democracy

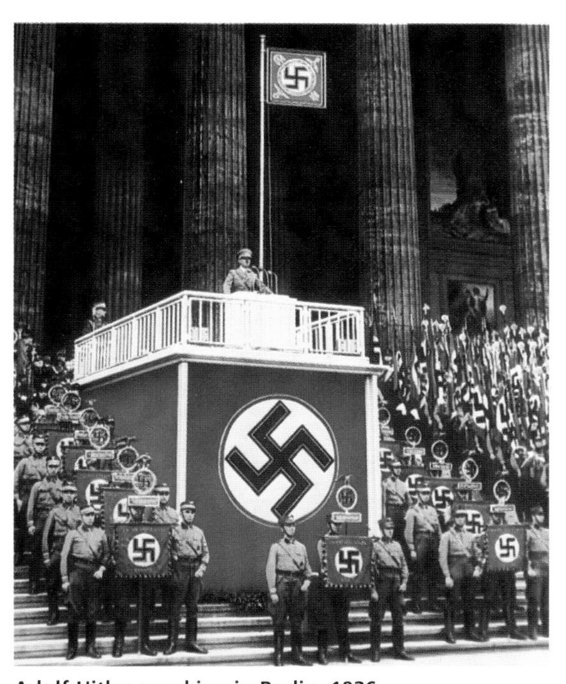

Adolf Hitler speaking in Berlin, 1936.

camps. At the same time, Hitler affirmed his determination to unite all German-speaking peoples and his intention to do so by force. He reestablished military service and started to rearm Germany.

Britain and France: democracies

Western Europe's two strongest democracies, Britain and France, underwent difficulties. Britain remained a parliamentary monarchy, with a king and a prime minister accountable to an elected parliament. The country had emerged weakened from the great war of 1914-1918 but still headed the largest colonial empire and retained an important place in the world. France possessed the world's second colonial empire. It was a republic with an elected president and a head of government responsible to a chamber of deputies. After the First World War, no French government managed to solve the country's economic and social problems. In 1934, after riots caused by the far right, the left-wing parties united in a "popular front," which won the 1936 elections. The new head of government, the socialist Léon Blum, passed important social laws: the workweek was limited to 40 hours and paid holidays were given for the first time. At the end of the 1930s, France and Britain seemed determined to safeguard peace. At the 1938 Munich conference, they allowed Hitler to annex a part of Czechoslovakia populated by Germans. A year later, the Second World War broke out. □

George VI, king of Great Britain from 1936 and during the Second World War. ▼

The Spanish Civil War ▲

In 1936, civil war broke out in Spain between the republican government supported by the USSR and the nationalists led by General Franco (above) and supported by Nazi Germany and fascist Italy. The fighting ended in 1939 with republican defeat. Franco became head of state and set up a dictatorship.

Dolores Ibarruri ▲

Known as "la Pasionaria," Dolores Ibarruri (1895-1989) was a famous opponent of General Franco. She was a member of the Spanish Communist Party, which during the Spanish Civil War, fought against the Falangists (supporters of Franco).

The main Asian countries underwent major changes between the wars. These were due to the struggle against British power in India and to political transformation in China and Japan.

Asia between

- **1919** April 13, India: massacre at Amritsar of supporters of Gandhi.
- **1921** China: founding of the Chinese Communist Party.
- **1922-1924** India: Gandhi is imprisoned.
- **1925** China: death of Sun Yat-sen.
- **1926** China: victory of Chiang Kai-shek. Japan: Hirohito becomes emperor.
- **1927** Japan: the military takes a key role in politics.
- **1930** April-March, India: Gandhi's March to the Sea.
- **1931** China and Japan: the Japanese invade Manchuria, in the north of China.
- **1934-1936** China: the Long March of Mao Zedong and the communists.
- **1935** India: New constitution introduced by the British.
- **1937** The Japanese invade China. Beginning of the war between Japan and China. Beijing captured by the Japanese.

In the first half of the 20th century, Asia experienced significant upheavals: Indians began to agitate for independence from Britain, China took a new political direction, and Japan came under the control of the military.

India

India had been part of the British empire, governed by a British viceroy, since the mid-19th century. Now more Indians began to follow Gandhi, an Indian lawyer educated in Britain, who wanted to achieve his country's independence by nonviolence. He incited the Indians to boycott British products, accepted imprisonment and staged hunger strikes to highlight his campaigns. To revive self-sufficiency and local textile crafts hit by competition from British mills, he encouraged others to follow his example of spinning cotton. The Indians called him Mahatma, the Great Soul. In 1919, a peaceful demonstration by Gandhi's supporters in Amritsar ended in violence as British soldiers killed several hundred Indians.

In 1930, Britain began negotiations to give India a new constitution. It was then that Gandhi organized the March to the Sea to demonstrate against the tax on salt: he and his followers distilled salt from sea water taken from the Arabian Sea. In 1935, a new constitution made India into a federation of eleven provinces and provided for the participation of Indians in their country's administration. However, nationalist agitation continued. A new nationalist leader, Nehru, replaced Gandhi in 1928 as the head of the nationalist Congress Party (see p. 81). In 1940, Muslims in India demanded the formation of a separate Muslim state.

China

In 1911, China became a republic, yet cities such as Shanghai were still controlled by Westerners. The republic's founder was Sun Yat-sen, who directed a revolutionary party, the Guomindang (see p. 79). He wanted to remove the foreigners and to reform China, but he governed only a small part of the country. Generals or warlords were the

◄ Mahatma Gandhi, in a procession in India.

Japan's emperor Hirohito and his staff.

the wars

Mao Zedong during the Long March in 1934.

real masters of many provinces. After Sun Yat-sen's death in 1925, the Guomindang split and Chiang Kai-shek, representing the more moderate branch, took power. Soon he was confronting the Chinese Communist Party, founded in Shanghai in 1921. The communists were led by Mao Zedong, Zhou Enlai and Zhu De. They were repressed in 1927, left Shanghai and first established themselves in the south of the country. Chiang Kai-shek tried to destroy them, so to avoid encirclement, Mao Zedong and Zhu De set out on the Long March. Across mountains and marshes, 130,000 people made a marathon trek of 12,000 km (7400 miles). Only 30,000 managed to reach Yenan in the north of China.

Japan

After the First World War, Japan occupied Germany's Pacific colonies and began to modernize its industry. In 1926, Emperor Hirohito succeeded his father as the ruler whom most Japanese regarded as a descendant of the gods. However, from 1927 onwards, the military played the key political role. The military maintained that Japan needed new lands and pushed for further military conquests. Secret nationalistic societies spread the idea of Japan's superiority over all other nations. In 1931 Japan invaded Manchuria, in the north of China, and created a dependent state called Manchukuo. In 1937, the Japanese invaded China itself, beginning a war that would last until the end of the Second World War in 1945. □

Turkey under Mustapha Kemal

Mustapha Kemal, who took the name of Atatürk, was a general and national hero who created the Turkish Republic in 1923, after the collapse of the Ottoman Empire. He became president and tried to make Turkey into a modern state. He instituted nonreligious education and the writing of Turkish in Latin rather than Arabic characters. In defiance of Islamic traditions, he made it obligatory for women to dress in Western fashion and forbade the wearing of the fez, the traditional male headdress. By so doing, he faced opposition from both the Kurds and the supporters of traditional Islam. He set up a strong one-party state, controlling public life, the press and the administration. Below, a Turkish woman greets Atatürk. ▼

In 1939, the Second World War began. Most countries became involved in a conflict that caused millions of deaths and left millions more as homeless refugees.

The Second World

1938 September: Hitler annexes part of Czechoslovakia.
1939 1 September: Hitler invades Poland. 3 September: Britain and France declare war on Germany.
1939-1940 The "Phony War."
1940 May: Germany invades the Netherlands, Belgium, Luxembourg and then France. 22 June: armistice between France and Germany. August-November: the Battle of Britain between German and British air forces.
1941 June: Germany invades the north of the USSR. 7 December: the Japanese attack the Americans at Pearl Harbor. The United States enters the war.
1942 June: American naval victory at Midway over Japan.
1943 February: the Germans are defeated by the Soviets at Stalingrad. 10 July: Allied landing in Sicily.
1944 6 June: D-Day, Allied landing in Normandy.
1945 May: the Soviets take Berlin. 8 May: capitulation of Germany. August: atomic bombs dropped on Hiroshima and Nagasaki; Japan capitulates.

Russian fighters on the roofs of Stalingrad in 1942.

The totalitarian regimes of Germany, Italy and Japan wanted to extend their domination over others. In 1938, to preserve peace, Britain and France accepted Germany's annexation of a part of Czechoslovakia. In May 1939, Hitler allied with Mussolini, and in August, he made a nonaggression pact with the USSR. In September, he invaded Poland. France and Britain then declared war on Germany.

The war in Europe (1939-1941)

In the east, the *Wehrmacht* (German army), using modern combat techniques with its *Panzers* (tanks) and air force, crushed Poland and divided it with the USSR. In the west, during the winter of 1939-1940, the French army waited, without taking the offensive. This was the Phony War. During this time, Germany occupied Denmark and Norway in *blitzkrieg* ("lightning war") attacks, while the USSR seized Finland. After invading the Netherlands, Belgium and Luxembourg, German troops advanced west with their armored forces into France through the Ardennes forest. This attack took the French and their British allies by surprise. They fell back, and most of the British troops had to be evacuated back to Britain from Dunkirk. In June 1940, Marshal Pétain of France signed an armistice with Germany, which put an end to the fighting in France, now mostly occupied by the Germans. Pétain became head of a French government installed at Vichy. Britain found itself alone against Hitler. There followed the Battle of Britain, air warfare between German and British

The air and sea battle of Midway, in the Pacific (June 1942).

War

aircraft that succeeded in preventing a German invasion of Britain. German bombers now targeted British cities and factories, but encouraged by prime minister Winston Churchill, the British fought on.

The war becomes worldwide (1941-1942)

Without declaring war, Germany and some of the countries that it controlled (Hungary, Romania, Finland) attacked the USSR in June 1941, with 4,000 tanks and 3,000 aircraft. The siege of Leningrad that began in September 1941 would last 900 days, and 800,000 Russians were to die of hunger and cold. In October 1941, the German army encircled Moscow but was forced to retreat in the face of heroic Soviet resistance. In North Africa, mainly in Italian-ruled Libya, the Germans and Italians fought the British. In the Pacific, the Japanese planned to create a "Great Eastern Asia," under their domination. However, such imperial schemes clashed with U.S. interests. In December 1941, the Japanese air force attacked the U.S. fleet based at Pearl Harbor in Hawaii and put it out of action. The United States entered the war, and by 1942, the conflict had become worldwide. The Axis powers (Germany, Italy, Japan and the countries they controlled) faced the Allies: Britain and its empire including Canada, Australia, New Zealand, South Africa and India; the United States; the USSR; as well as other nations. The Allies were aided by resistance movements in the occupied countries. Europe, the Pacific and North Africa were all involved in the fighting.

ding of Allied troops in Normandy, 6 June 1944.

The end of the war (1942-1945)

In 1942, the tide turned in the Allies' favor. The Americans won the battle of Midway and reconquered the principal Pacific islands. The Allies landed in Morocco and Algeria and defeated the Italians and Germans, whom they drove out of Tunisia. In February 1943, a German army capitulated in the USSR at Stalingrad. The landing of the Allies in Sicily and Italy brought down Mussolini in July 1943. On 6 June 1944, in a coordinated military operation, the Allies landed in Normandy, France. In 1945, after hard fighting, they entered Germany from the west. The USSR's Red Army from the east was first to reach Berlin. Hitler committed suicide on 30 April, and Germany surrendered on 8 May 1945. In the Pacific, the United States used the new weapon, the atomic bomb, in August 1945 to destroy the Japanese cities of Hiroshima and Nagasaki. Japan then surrendered. □

Europe in 1942

In 1942, many countries had been defeated by Germany and the countries that it controlled. Only Britain and the USSR still resisted.

Germany and occupied countries

German allies and countries under its control

Countries at war with Germany

Neutral states

The war in the Pacific

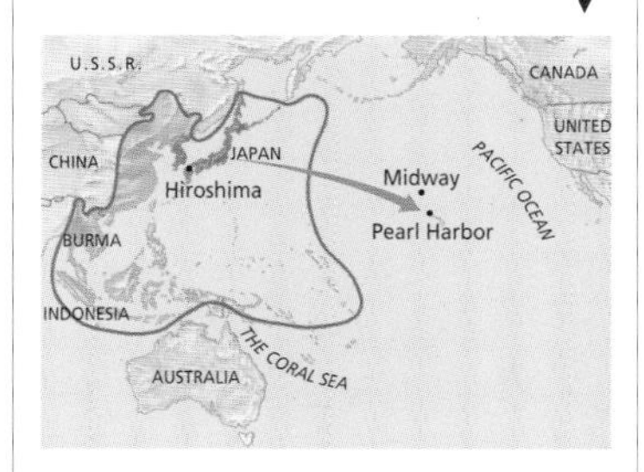

The Japanese were masters of eastern China. They also occupied Indonesia and the other Asian colonies of the allied countries, apart from India. The defeat at Midway against the Americans, in June 1942, marked the end of the Japanese advance in Asia.

Jewish families of the Warsaw ghetto in Poland being taken to concentration camps in 1942.

Civilians in the war

The Jewish star

Hitler and the Nazis considered the "Aryan" ancestors of the Germans to be a race superior to all others and the Jews as an inferior race. In 1933, the Nazis organized boycotts of Jewish shops in Germany, and the first concentration camp was set up. In 1935, Hitler passed laws (the Nuremberg laws) against the Jews. They were excluded from higher education and many professions. Their goods were confiscated. They were prohibited from public places. They were forced to wear a yellow star marked with the word *Jude* (German for "Jew"). During the Second World War, the persecution of the Jews spread throughout Europe. In central Europe, they were forced to live in separate districts called ghettos. After 1942, they were sent to extermination camps.

During the Second World War, civilians in Europe and in Asia suffered a great deal. Everyday life was difficult, especially in the occupied countries where some people joined forces to resist the occupying armies and formed resistance networks. In all the countries that they occupied, the Nazis carried out systematic deportation of the Jews.

Daily life

When Germany in 1940 invaded the Netherlands, Belgium, Luxembourg and then France, many people fled south to escape the enemy. Roads were packed with nearly 10 million civilians fleeing on foot, on bicycles and in cars. In the territories that they occupied, German troops seized factories and factory goods, farm crops and livestock, coal and minerals. In the countries at war, food and everyday necessities were rationed: people could buy only small quantities in exchange for coupons issued by the government. Some people resorted to the black market, paying high prices in secret for goods whose sale was prohibited. Civilians were also subject to torture, looting, imprisonment, execution and other forms of violent repression. They also suffered from aerial bombardment: the *Luftwaffe* (German air force) destroyed Warsaw, Rotterdam, Belgrade and large parts of London. In response, the Allies bombed cities controlled by Germany, including Caen, Le Havre and Brest in France. Three-quarters of Dresden in Germany was destroyed by bombs in February 1945, and 250,000 of its inhabitants were killed. In Asia, the Japanese occupation of Burma, Malaysia, Indonesia and the Philippines was just as destructive.

◄ **The German city of Dresden was destroyed by Allied bombing in 1945.**

Russian partisans during a sabotage operation in 1942.

Auschwitz extermination camp.

Prisoners in a concentration camp.

Collaboration and resistance

In the occupied countries, some groups collaborated with the Nazis—for example, the Croat Ustashas in Yugoslavia and the Belgian Rexist party. Some governments also collaborated—Quisling's government in Norway and the French administration headed by Marshal Pétain at Vichy. However, resistance was gradually organized. Anti-Nazi broadcasts to the European countries were sent out from Britain by the BBC. These broadcasts were listened to in secret and encouraged resistance against occupation and collaboration. From 1940, resistance fighters sabotaged railways and factories in occupied countries, set up information networks and organized armed underground groups. Soviet and Yugoslav partisans were among the most active resistance fighters. In 1944, the Polish resistance staged an insurrection in Warsaw, a year after the April 1943 ghetto rising. In France, the resistance movements were gradually united by Jean Moulin under the direction of General Charles de Gaulle, leader of the Free French in Britain.

Concentration camps

The Nazis believed that the Jews threatened the purity of the Germanic race and decided to exterminate them. In 1933, the first concentration camp was built at Dachau to imprison the Jews and opponents of the regime, especially communists. After 1941, extermination camps were set up in which prisoners were killed en masse. In 1942, the Nazi leaders decided to embark on the "final solution," the genocide (systematic destruction of a people) of all the Jews of Europe. They organized massive sweeps, such as those in Warsaw and Paris during the summer of 1942, to arrest Jewish families. Packed into freight trains that brought them to the extermination camps, the Jews were to die in gas chambers, their bodies burned in incinerators. In some camps, healthy prisoners were used as forced labor: dressed in striped uniforms, tattooed with a number on their forearm, these starving prisoners were tortured and often worked to death. Resistance fighters, gypsies, Slavs (Russians and Poles) and homosexuals were also sent to concentration camps. Roughly a thousand death camps were set up across Europe, in which more than 5 million Jews died, together with another 2 million prisoners. □

The atomic bomb

On 6 August 1945, the Americans dropped an atomic bomb on the Japanese city of Hiroshima, hoping to defeat the Japanese definitively. It was the first time atomic weapons were ever used. Of Hiroshima's 330,000 inhabitants, 80,000 were killed and 70,000 were injured. The entire center of the city, where temperatures reached 10,832°F at the bomb's point of impact, was destroyed, and no one survived within a radius of about 1,640 feet. Then on 9 August, the Americans destroyed another city, Nagasaki, with another atomic bomb. On 15 August, Japan surrendered. Many of the two cities' inhabitants died years later of cancers and other ailments caused by the two bombs. Use of the atomic bomb had forever changed the way governments thought about armed conflicts. ▼

After the Second World War, the world divided into two blocks dominated by the USSR and the USA. Former colonies achieved their independence and sought to stay nonaligned between these Cold War rivals.

The postwar world

1945 Yalta conference between Churchill, Roosevelt and Stalin. Founding of the United Nations.
1945 17 July-2 August: Potsdam conference between the Americans, British and Russians.
1947 The Americans offer Europe a plan for economic reconstruction: the Marshall Plan. Independence of India; beginning of decolonization in Asia.
1948 Czechoslovakia becomes communist.
1949 Setting up of NATO (the North Atlantic Treaty Organization). Creation of the German Federal Republic (West) and the German Democratic Republic (East). Communist victory in China, which becomes a people's republic.
1950-1953 Korean War between North Korea and South Korea.
1955 Afro-Asian conference at Bandung. Creation of the Warsaw Pact.
1961 13 August: Building of the Berlin Wall.
1962 The USSR sets up missiles on Cuba; U.S. president John F. Kennedy threatens to use atomic weapons against the Russians, who back down.
1975 By now, almost all Africa is decolonized.

Churchill, Roosevelt and Stalin at the Yalta Conference of 1945.

One of the important consequences of the Second World War was the division of the world into two spheres of influence. One was dominated by the USSR, a communist country in which the state directed the economy. The other was led by the United States, a capitalist country with a free market economy dependent on private property and individual action. Independence gradually won by the colonies of European countries was the other major development in the postwar world.

East and West

In February 1945, U.S. president Roosevelt, British prime minister Churchill and Soviet leader Stalin met at Yalta, in the Crimea, to organize postwar Europe. The United Nations, intended to safeguard peace, was then founded. Some months later at Potsdam in Germany, the representatives of the three countries agreed to four occupation zones in defeated Germany: American, British, French and Soviet. The city of Berlin, in the center of the Soviet zone, was itself divided in four. The USSR and the USA reinforced their influence over the parts of the world that they dominated. Two blocs formed. The Eastern bloc comprised the USSR and the countries it controlled, Bulgaria, Romania, Poland, Hungary and Czechoslovakia after a communist coup in 1948. Yugoslavia, a communist country, rejected the USSR's control. The Western bloc included the United States and the European countries to which it lent economic aid through the Marshall Plan for reconstruction. In 1949, NATO (the North Atlantic Treaty Organization), a military alliance that linked the United States and Canada with the countries of Western Europe, enabled the Americans to move nuclear weapons into Europe. In 1955, the Eastern bloc also created a military organization—the Warsaw Pact. From this point, Europe was divided between these two rival blocs with only one or two nations (such as Sweden and Switzerland) staying neutral.

Border checkpoint of the American zone in Berlin, 1946.

The Cold War

The name Cold War refers to the struggle between the USSR and the USA that was waged without the two superpowers ever coming into direct combat. Their first confrontation was in Europe. In 1948, the USSR threatened Berlin in a crisis that led to the creation, in 1949, of two German states: the German Federal Republic (GFR), allied to the countries of the West, and the German Democratic Republic (GDR), under Soviet control. Asia was the second confrontation zone. In 1949, Chinese communists proclaimed the People's Republic of China. In 1950, the communists of North Korea, supported by China and the USSR, invaded South Korea, to which the UN sent troops under American command. At the end of the Korean War in 1953, the country remained divided into North Korea and South Korea. From 1956, American and Soviet leaders talked of disarmament but tension continued. During the night of 12 August 1961, the East German authorities began to build a wall to prevent East Germans from moving to the West. In 1962, U.S. president John F. Kennedy threatened to use atomic weapons against the USSR, which had built missile bases on Cuba, a communist country close to the USA. This event is considered one of the key points of the Cold War.

In Africa, Senegalese celebrate independence in 1958. ▼

Decolonization

Before 1940, most European countries had overseas colonies, mainly in Asia and Africa. After the war, these colonies gradually achieved their independence. In some countries, independence was agreed between the colonized and the colonizers, as occurred between India and Ceylon (now Sri Lanka) and Britain, and in French black Africa. In other countries, wars of liberation were fought: in Indonesia against the Netherlands, in Indochina and Algeria against France, in Mozambique against Portugal. By the end of the 1950s, all of Asia had obtained independence. By the end of the 1960s, almost all of Africa was independent. The new nations emphasized their distinctiveness at the Bandung Conference in 1955 and strove to take up a position between the two blocs as a third force in world affairs. □

The United Nations ▲

In 1945, the Allies created the United Nations Organization, intended to safeguard peace and to promote economic, social and cultural cooperation between nations.

The Bandung Conference

In 1955, the Bandung Conference in Indonesia brought the heads of state of African and Asian countries, including President Sukarno (below) of Indonesia and Prime Ministers Nasser of Egypt and Nehru of India. The conference condemned colonialism. ▼

After 1945, China became a people's republic and Japan experienced extraordinary economic growth. The newly independent countries of Southeast Asia adopted different economic systems.

East Asia: China

- **1946-1954** War in Indochina between the Vietnamese communists, who demand independence, and France.
- **1947** Independence of India: partition of India and Pakistan.
- **1949** Independence of Indonesia.
- **1949** 1 October: Proclamation of the People's Republic of China.
- **1955-1975** Vietnam war between communist North Vietnam and South Vietnam supported by the United States.
- **1958** China: beginning of the "Great Leap Forward."
- **1965** Singapore becomes an independent republic.
- **1966** China: beginning of the Cultural Revolution.
- **1967** India: Indira Gandhi becomes prime minister.
- **1971** Creation of the state of Bangladesh, from former East Pakistan.
- **1975-1979** Cambodia: dictatorship of the Khmer Rouge.
- **1976** China: death of Mao Zedong.
- **1977** China: Deng Xiaoping comes to power.
- **1984** India: assassination of Indira Gandhi by religious extremists.
- **1989** China: the army attacks pro-democracy demonstrators in Beijing.
- **1997** Death of Deng Xiaoping.

Two nations dominate modern East Asia: China, which became communist in 1949 and has the world's largest population, and Japan, which has developed on the capitalist model and become one of the world's leading economic powers.

Mao's China

In China, after the Second World War, the Guomindang nationalists and the communists renewed their struggle (see p. 94-95). The conflict ended in 1949 with communist victory: the People's Republic of China was proclaimed and Mao Zedong became its first leader. The country was in ruins after forty years of unrest. Adopting the Soviet model, the communists set up an authoritarian regime and made far-reaching reforms. Industry was modernized and reorganized. Millions of people, in particular rich landowners, were arrested and many were executed. Some Chinese remained hostile to communism. From 1958, Mao began to move away from the Soviet model, launching a reform he called the "Great Leap Forward," to produce instantly a new communist society. In the countryside, "people's communes" were set up formed of families who worked the land in common and shared agricultural and industrial work. The commune was responsible for everything: health, political instruction, education of children, and so on. However, the Great Leap Forward did not bring all the desired advances. In 1966, relying on the army and on young people, Mao unleashed the Cultural Revolution. For three years, "Red Guards," groups of young fanatics, harassed anyone who held some authority (teachers, intellectuals, civil servants). Referring to the "Little Red Book," which contained the thoughts of Chairman Mao, they instituted a reign of terror, destroying all books and works of art that were reminders of pre-communist China. The Cultural Revolution lasted for nearly ten years and caused several million deaths.

Mao Zedong and China's defense minister Lin Biao in 1959. ▼

Young Pioneers involved in China's Cultural Revolution, 1966-1976.

and Japan

U.S. general MacArthur and Japanese Emperor Hirohito in Tokyo.

China today

Mao died in 1976, and in the following year, Deng Xiaoping came to power. Deng set in motion a program to modernize industry, agriculture, the army and sciences. China gradually liberalized, and private companies, commerce, banks and trade with other countries developed. However, the political system did not change and remains dominated by the Communist Party, which allows no opposition. In May 1989, students occupied Tiananmen Square in Beijing to demand more freedom. On 4 June, the government sent in the army, which attacked the students, killing several hundred.

Japan from the war to the present

In 1945, Japan emerged from the war defeated and weak. More than 2 million Japanese had died, and half the country's cities were destroyed. Japan had also lost its colonies: Korea, the south of the island of Sakhalin and Taiwan. An American army commanded by General MacArthur occupied the country, on which a new, more democratic constitution was imposed. Hirohito remained emperor but lost a great deal of his power. He remained titular head of the country until his death in 1989. Within a few years, however, Japan made an extraordinary economic recovery to become a leading nation in the world economy, especially in the electronics, car, computer and robotics industries. Japan has become a growth model for other Asian countries, in particular for those countries with a high economic growth rate (the so-called dragon or tiger economies) such as South Korea, Taiwan, Singapore and Hong Kong. Japan is now one of the world's leading economic powers. □

The stock exchange of Tokyo, Japan's capital, in 1987.

North Korea and South Korea

From 1948, Korea has been divided between communist North Korea—once supported by the USSR and China—and South Korea, backed by the United States. The Korean War between the North and South lasted from 1950 to 1953. The country remains divided.

Since then, South Korea (capital: Seoul) has followed the Japanese example in industrial development and increased its production. It has become one of the most dynamic countries in Asia. ▲

North Korea (capital: Pyongyang) was ruled from 1948 to 1994 by Kim Il-Sung (above). He developed the country on rigid old-style Soviet lines. ▲

An Indian city in 1990.

India and Southeast Asia

The Philippines

The Philippines, a state of many islands in Southeast Asia, has a turbulent history. First visited by Magellan in 1521, the islands were colonized by Spain until the end of the 19th century and then ceded to the United States. From 1941 to 1945, the country was occupied by the Japanese. The independent Republic of the Philippines, formed in 1946, remained under American influence. Elected president of the Republic in 1965, Ferdinand Marcos set up a dictatorship. In 1983, Corazon Aquino (above, greeting supporters) became leader of the opposition in place of her assassinated husband. She was elected president of the republic in 1986, and Marcos was forced into exile. However, Aquino faced several attempted challenges and after the 1992 elections she was succeeded by general Fidel Ramos.

Modern India, Pakistan, Sri Lanka, Burma and the countries of Southeast Asia (Vietnam, Laos, Cambodia, Indonesia, the Philippines and Malaysia) all gained independence after the Second World War. These states were former British, Dutch, American or French colonies.

India, Pakistan, Bangladesh

Negotiations between the Indian nationalists and the British government, begun before the Second World War, were completed in 1947. India became independent but was divided into two states: the Republic of India, mainly populated by Hindus; and Pakistan, which is mainly Muslim. Other British possessions obtained their independence: Ceylon (modern Sri Lanka) in 1947 and Burma (now Myanmar) in 1948. The development of independent India was led by the national leader Jawaharlal Nehru. Prime minister from 1947 to 1964, he attempted to suppress the caste system (see *Religions of the World*). Thanks to his efforts, and those of his daughter Indira Gandhi, who became prime minister in 1967, India modernized its industry and increased its agricultural production (the "green revolution") by encouraging the peasants to use fertilizers and improved seed. However, difficulties remain, in particular a rapidly growing population and wide gap between rich and poor. The governments of the Indian subcontinent have faced problems posed by often violent confrontations between different religious groups. In 1947, Pakistan came into being as two separated provinces, East Pakistan and West Pakistan, with M.A. Jinnah as head of state. In 1971, East Pakistan broke away to form the republic of Bangladesh. After a period of military dictatorship, Benazir Bhutto became leader of Pakistan in 1988—the first woman to reach such a position in a Muslim state. She resigned in 1990, but she returned to power from 1993 to 1996.

Southeast Asia

Thailand has never been colonized. Indonesia, a Dutch colony, proclaimed its independence in 1945 but was not recognized until 1949, after a war waged by the National Party led by Sukarno. Sukarno set up a republic of which

Nehru in 1947 with Lord Mountbatten, the last British viceroy of India, and Jinnah.

American soldiers during the Vietnam War.

The Chinese quarter of Hanoi, capital of Vietnam.

he was the first president. Malaysia became independent in 1957, and Singapore in 1965. The other countries of Southeast Asia also achieved independence in the 1950s.

Vietnam, Cambodia and Laos

French Indochina was made up of present-day Vietnam, Cambodia and Laos. Decolonization took place not by agreement, as in India, but only through the Indochina War (1946-1954) fought between the Vietnamese communists and the French. In 1953, Cambodia and Laos achieved their independence. In 1954, Vietnam was divided into two independent states: communist North Vietnam ruled by Ho Chi Minh and South Vietnam. Soon these two countries were at war. The United States sent large numbers of troops to help South Vietnam but could not end the conflict. In 1975, communist troops from the North captured Saigon, capital of South Vietnam, reunifying the country, and set up a communist regime. To escape the communists, thousands of people risked their lives by putting to sea in small craft. When these "boat people" reached neighboring countries (Malaysia, Thailand, the Philippines), most were put in refugee camps. Also in 1975, the communist Khmer Rouge took power in Cambodia and set up a cruel and violent dictatorship in which millions of people were massacred, tortured or made to do forced labor. The political situation has been calmer since 1989. Today, Vietnam and Cambodia, which are still very poor, are trying to improve their economies. □

Cambodians in a refugee camp. ▼

Australia ▲

The former British colonies of Australia united in 1901 to form a federal state. Australians fought in the two world wars on the side of the Allies. This continent in the Pacific Ocean had traditional links with Britain but is now building closer ties with its Asian neighbors and with the United States. Above, Sydney Opera House, built in 1967.

Singapore

In 1965, Singapore separated from Malaysia and became independent. More than 3 million people, mostly Chinese, live on this small but wealthy island. The country's prosperity is based on trade, and its government rule is strict. ▼

After the Second World War, the State of Israel was created. The Middle East became a scene of confrontation between Israel and the Arab countries and a testing ground for the superpowers.

The Middle East

- **1945** Founding of the Arab League.
- **1948** Declaration of the State of Israel. First Arab-Israeli war.
- **1952** Nasser overthrows the monarchy in Egypt.
- **1956** Second Arab-Israeli war.
- **1964** Creation of the PLO (Palestine Liberation Organization).
- **1967** June: Third Arab-Israeli war (Six-Day War).
- **1973** October: fourth Arab-Israeli war.
- **1974** Speech of Yasser Arafat at the UN: the UN recognizes the PLO.
- **1975-1990** Civil war in Lebanon.
- **1978** Camp David Accords signed between Egypt and Israel.
- **1979** Islamic republic formed in Iran.
- **1987** Beginning of Palestinian uprising in the occupied territories.
- **1991** Gulf War between Iraq and Kuwait, with the United States and many other countries intervening.
- **1993** 13 September: peace agreements signed between Yasser Arafat and Yitzhak Rabin.

The Middle East is a region with imprecise geographical limits. It includes the Arab countries (Iraq, the Gulf states, Saudi Arabia, Jordan, Syria, Lebanon and Egypt), as well as Iran and Israel.

Israel and Palestine

Zionism, a movement to reunite Jews scattered across the world, had been campaigning since the 19th century for a Jewish state in Palestine where the ancestors of the Jews lived since ancient times. Arabs had been settled in this region since the 7th century. In 1917, the British government supported the creation in Palestine of a national homeland for the Jewish people, and in the 1930s growing numbers of Jewish colonists settled there. Tension then increased between the Jews and the Arabs. After the Second World War, Palestine appeared to be a refuge for survivors of the Nazi genocide against the Jews. In 1947, the UN decided to divide Palestine into a Jewish state and an Arab state. The Arab countries rejected this division, but the Jews proclaimed the State of Israel in 1948 with David Ben-Gurion heading the provisional government. Israel was rapidly settled by Jews arriving from at least 74 different countries. The Arab countries attacked the new state, setting off the first of the Arab-Israeli wars, which ended in 1949 with victory for Israel. The United States supported the Israeli cause. The Arab states and the USSR took up the cause of the Palestinians, the Arabs living in Israel. In 1956, Israel won a second war, and in 1967 it was again victorious in the Six-Day War. Israel then occupied Arab territories (Sinai, the Gaza Strip, the West Bank and the Golan Heights), although the UN ordered it to withdraw from them. When Israel was founded, many Palestinians were forced into exile in other countries, which put them in refugee camps. In 1964, they created the PLO (Palestine Liberation Organization), led since 1969 by Yasser Arafat.

A young Palestinian during the *Intifada* or uprising of 1988.

Israeli soldier during the Six-Day War of 1967. ▶

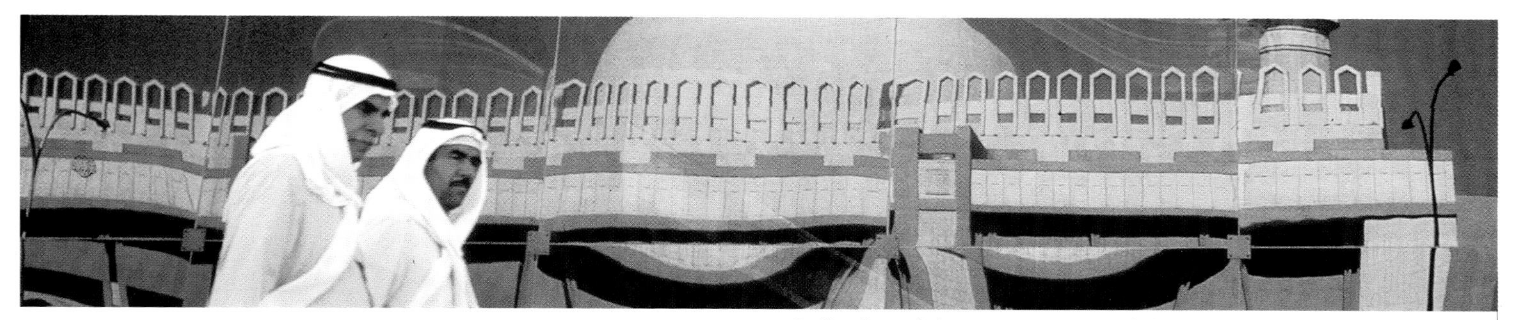

Reflection of the Great Mosque of the State on a building in Kuwait.

From war to peace

In October 1973, Egypt and Syria attacked Israel. The Israelis at first retreated but then won the war. The Egyptian president, Anwar Sadat, proposed peace talks to the Israelis, and agreements were signed at Camp David in the United States in 1978. Another consequence of the 1973 war was a sharp increase in oil prices, imposed by the Arab countries on the Western countries that supported Israel. The PLO conducted a terrorist campaign (airliner hijackings and bombings) against Israel and the states that it claimed supported Israel. In 1987, young Palestinians in the occupied territories launched a new form of war, the *Intifada* ("uprising" in Arabic), harassing the Israeli army with stone-throwing and other acts of violence. However, a peace process continued slowly. In 1974, the UN recognized the PLO. In 1991, the Palestinians and the Arab countries took part with Israel in a peace conference. In 1993, after long negotiations organized by the Americans, the Israeli prime minister Yitzhak Rabin and Yasser Arafat signed peace agreements. In 1994, the Palestinian National Authority, headed by Yasser Arafat, was set up in Gaza and several towns on the West Bank.

Yitzhak Rabin, U.S. President Bill Clinton and Yasser Arafat at the 1993 Israel-PLO agreement. ▼

The Arab countries, Iran and Islam

The Arab countries of the Middle East have common interests. To demonstrate their independence from the great powers, they founded the Arab League in 1945. But disagreements have also arisen, in particular between the countries with immense reserves of oil, such as Saudi Arabia, and those like Egypt and Syria, which have little oil wealth. Lebanon was ravaged by a civil war from 1975 to 1990. In 1990, the Iraqis, led by Saddam Hussein, occupied neighboring Kuwait, starting the Gulf War in which the United States and many other countries intervened. The Arab countries of the Middle East are united by a single religion, Islam. From 1927, the "Muslim Brotherhood" in Egypt affirmed that followers of Islam must apply in full the *sharia*, the law of the Koran. Such fundamentalists reject ideas from the non-Muslim world, especially Europe and America. Islamic fundamentalism was strengthened in 1979 by the coming to power in Iran of Ayatollah Khomeini, a religious leader who set up a very strict Islamic republic. In almost all Arab countries, fundamentalist groups are fighting to impose their regime and carrying out terrorist actions to further their aim. □

Egypt ▲

To Egyptians (above), Gamal Abdel Nasser (below, in 1956) is a hero. From a peasant family, he became an army officer and took part in the 1952 coup d'état that overthrew King Farouk, who had been backed by the British. From 1954 until his death in 1970, Nasser governed Egypt. In 1956, he regained from the British and French the Suez Canal, which has since then belonged to Egypt. This success made him a symbol for Arab nationalism and anti-colonialism. ▼

From 1955 to 1965, almost all Africa became independent. After decolonization, most African states encountered political and economic difficulties, which they strove to overcome.

Africa

- **1954-1962 Algeria: Algerian nationalists fight against the French government. In April 1962, Algeria becomes independent.**
- **1956 Independence of Tunisia, Morocco and Sudan.**
- **1957 Independence of Ghana.**
- **1960 The French colonies in black Africa achieve independence. The British colony of Nigeria and the Belgian Congo (now called the Democratic Republic of Zaire) become independent.**
- **1961 Morocco: Hassan II becomes king.**
- **1975 Independence of Angola and Mozambique.**
- **1976 South Africa: bloody suppression of Soweto riots.**
- **1984-85 Famine in Ethiopia.**
- **1990 Independence of Namibia.**
- **1991 South Africa: the three remaining laws enforcing apartheid are abolished.**
- **1994 Rwanda: civil war between the Hutu and the Tutsi.**
- **1994 South Africa; victory of the ANC in the country's first multiracial elections; Nelson Mandela is elected president.**

After the Second World War, the colonies of Africa gradually became independent, either by agreement or through armed struggle. The movement toward decolonization affected almost the whole of Africa in the years from 1955 to 1965. However, most new African states remained indirectly dominated by, or dependent on, Western states and experienced serious political and economic difficulties. Wars and natural disasters such as severe drought caused major famines, for example, in Biafra from 1967-1970, in Ethiopia in 1973 and again in 1984-85, in Somalia in 1991 and in other regions of Africa.

Chadli Ben Djedid, the Algerian president, and Habib Bourguiba, Tunisia's president, in 1983.

North Africa: Morocco, Tunisia, Algeria

The countries of the Maghreb (Morocco, Tunisia, Algeria), which were French colonies, became independent between 1956 and 1962. Morocco's independence was proclaimed in 1956; in 1957, the country became a kingdom governed by Mohammed V and, after his death in 1961, by his son Hassan II. Hassan hoped to form a Greater Maghreb with Algeria and Tunisia but faced considerable opposition. In Tunisia, a republic was proclaimed in 1957 by Habib Bourguiba, who became its elected president and set up a relatively liberal regime. He became president for life in 1975 and was overthrown in 1987 by his prime minister Ben Ali, who since then has worked to make Tunisia more democratic, opposing Islamic extremists. Algeria achieved its independence after the Algerian war, 1954-1962, fought between Algerian nationalists and the French government. Ahmed Ben Bella became president of the new republic and began socialist reforms, setting up a regime aligned with the USSR. In 1965, he was overthrown by Boumediene, who remained neutral between the United States and the USSR. After his death in 1979, his successor was Chadli Ben Djedid, the only candidate in the elections. Since 1991, Algeria has experienced an upsurge in Islamic extremism.

West and Central Africa

Almost all the colonies of western and central Africa achieved their independence between 1955 to 1965. The new states were faced with many political difficulties. There were stable regimes, like those headed by Félix Houphouët-Boigny, president of the Ivory Coast from 1960 until his death in 1993, or Léopold Senghor, president of Senegal from 1960 to 1980. However, many countries had problems in developing their economies and feeding rapidly growing populations. Through the military, technical and food aid which they supply, many foreign countries heavily influence African governments. Moreover, the frontiers drawn by the Europeans during colonization did not take into account different ethnic divisions. Since independence, civil wars between opposing

Young Algerians in 1987.

F. W. De Klerk, president of South Africa, and Nelson Mandela, leader of the ANC, in 1992.

ethnic groups have been frequent. Confrontations between the Hutu and the Tutsi turned Rwanda into a bloodbath in 1994. Yet, in spite of these problems, since 1990 most authoritarian states have been evolving, if at times with difficulty, toward democracy.

Southern Africa

In the south of the African continent, the Union of South Africa became a republic in 1961. It was barred from the British Commonwealth while successive governments continued the policy of apartheid (racial segregation or separation of the races), despite condemnation from other countries. The African National Congress (ANC), led by Nelson Mandela, supported campaigns of resistance by blacks against apartheid. Other countries in southern Africa supported the ANC. Angola and Mozambique, former Portuguese colonies that became independent in 1975, were torn apart by civil wars. South Africa intervened in the Angolan war until 1988. From 1990, major changes began to occur. Namibia became independent. In 1990, F. W. De Klerk became president of South Africa and released Nelson Mandela after twenty-seven years of imprisonment. The last laws enforcing apartheid were abolished. In 1994, the ANC won the country's first multiracial elections and Mandela became president of South Africa. □

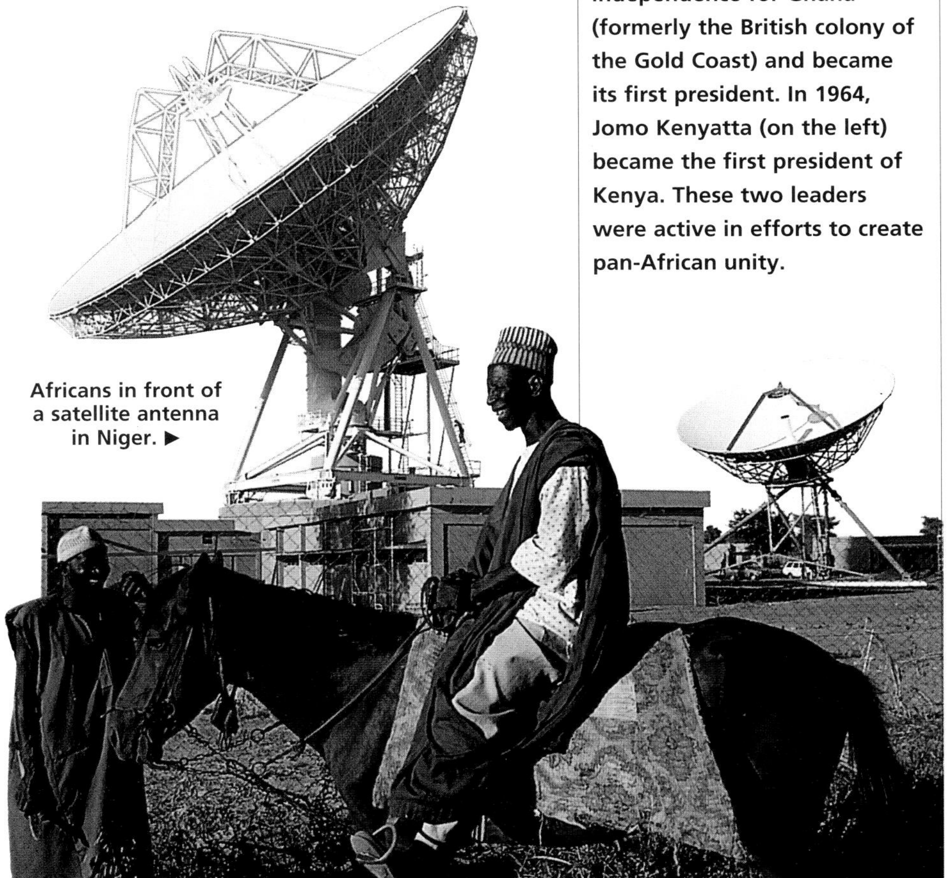

Africans in front of a satellite antenna in Niger. ▶

Jomo Kenyatta and Kwame Nkrumah ▲

In 1957, Kwame Nkrumah (on the right) gained independence for Ghana (formerly the British colony of the Gold Coast) and became its first president. In 1964, Jomo Kenyatta (on the left) became the first president of Kenya. These two leaders were active in efforts to create pan-African unity.

The United States as the world's leading power exercises influence over many countries in Latin America. The states of Latin America are making efforts to assert their independence from their powerful neighbor.

The Americas

1946 Argentina: Juan Perón is elected president.
1950-1954 United States: Senator Joseph McCarthy leads a campaign against communists.
1959 Cuba: Fidel Castro takes power.
1963 August, United States: march by blacks on Washington.
1963 November, United States: assassination of John F. Kennedy in Dallas.
1968 United States: assassination of Martin Luther King in Memphis.
1969 Two Americans walk on the moon.
1973 Chile: Allende is overthrown by the dictator Pinochet.
1982 Canada: the constitution becomes a solely Canadian responsibility.
1983 Argentina: end of the military dictatorship, Raul Alfonsín becomes president.
1991 The United States leads the allies in the Gulf War.

Since 1945, the United States has maintained its position as the leading world power. Canada, in the north of the American continent, broke its last constitutional link with Britain in the 1980s.

The United States, a world power

The United States has powerful armed forces and weapons and vast financial resources, and has made great technological advances in aviation, shipping and industry. It is a rich country, wielding influence over a large part of the world. The American way of life has become a model for many people: for example, high-rise cities and a wide range of consumer goods (products used in daily life). As leader of the Western bloc (see p. 100-101), the United States worked to prevent communism from spreading abroad and within its frontiers. From 1950 to 1954, under presidents Truman and Eisenhower, Senator Joseph McCarthy led a national campaign against communists. Elected president in 1960, the Democrat John F. Kennedy sought to give his country a new boost and proposed two major objectives: greater social justice and the conquest of space. He was assassinated in 1963. In 1969, two American astronauts, Neil Armstrong and Edwin Aldrin, walked on the moon.

John F. Kennedy and his wife in New York during the 1960 election campaign.

Difficult years

The southern states of the USA practiced racial segregation—organized and regulated separation of blacks and whites in schools and public places. From 1955, the black Baptist minister Martin Luther King Jr. campaigned for civil rights for black Americans. In 1957, riots broke out in Little Rock, Arkansas, during desegregation of the schools. In 1963, with support from President Kennedy, several thousand blacks organized a march on Washington. A civil-rights law guaranteeing a number of rights to blacks was passed in 1964. However, protests continued. The Black Muslim leader Malcolm X was assassinated in 1965 and Martin Luther King Jr. in 1968. In the 1960s, student protest movements rose up against mainstream American society that to some seemed based on money and consumption. Students also opposed the sending of troops to Vietnam (see p. 105). Increasing numbers of other Americans denounced this war as unjustified. In 1973, under President Richard Nixon, the Americans withdrew from Vietnam. The Vietnam War, in which 50,000 U.S. soldiers died and tens of thousands were wounded, had traumatized the country.

Skyscrapers of Manhattan, New York City.

Martin Luther King Jr. in 1963.

The United States today

In the 1970s, disarmament talks were started with the USSR. At the same period, the United States went through a serious crisis linked to the rise in the price of oil (see p. 107). In 1974, the Watergate scandal broke when the Republican president, Nixon, was accused of knowing about an illegal entry into the Watergate building, headquarters of the Democratic party. Nixon was forced to resign. In the 1980s, under Ronald Reagan's presidency, the number of unemployed and poor increased, as in many other developed countries. In industry, the Japanese competed successfully with the Americans, especially in the car and computer sectors. However, the U.S. economy recovered, and at the turn of the millennium, the United States is still the world's richest and most powerful state.

Canada

From 1948, Canada began to develop a policy of alignment with the United States. In 1982, it broke the last official link with Great Britain: from then on its constitution was alterable only by the Canadian government. Canada is made up of ten provinces and three territories. The central government exercises authority over the provinces, which have their own governments, which tend to seek more power and money to apply their own programs. Quebec, the only majority French-speaking province of Canada, has a separatist movement demanding a unique status and even independence. The American Indians and the Inuit (the country's original inhabitants) have recently won greater respect for their ancestral rights and more autonomy. On 1 April 1999, the eastern section of the Northwest Territories was turned into a separate territory, Nunavut ("our land" in Inuktitut, the language spoken by the Inuit.) Its population of 25,000 is 85 percent Inuit and will be self-governing. □

Vancouver, a great Canadian city ▲

Vancouver, in the province of British Columbia, is Canada's third city, with more than 1.4 million inhabitants. Founded at the end of the 19th century, it is a modern city with a distinctive style of architecture. It owes its rapid growth to the railway and its privileged position on the Pacific Ocean, which makes it the country's leading port.

◄ The American software magnate, Bill Gates.

Mexico City, capital of Mexico.

Latin America

Juan and Eva Perón ▲

From a modest background, Eva Perón was a support to her husband, who ruled Argentina beginning in 1946. She was extremely popular and urged Juan Perón to extend the vote to women and legalize divorce.

Colombia

Coffee (below) has for many years been the principal resource of Colombia, currently in heavy debt.

During the years from 1950 to 1970, the countries of Latin America experienced mixed fortunes. Long dependent on the United States both economically and politically, they attempted to break free from its dominance.

The Cuban revolution

Cuba's dictator, Fulgencio Batista, held power from 1952 with the support of the United States. Fidel Castro and Ernesto "Che" Guevara were organizers of a revolutionary guerrilla movement that in 1959 drove Batista from power and set up a communist regime led by Castro. In 1961, the anti-Castro landing of Cuban exiles at the Bay of Pigs was repulsed. In 1962, the Soviets set up missiles on Cuba that threatened the United States, but they were finally forced to withdraw (see p. 101). The Cuban government inspired and helped revolutionaries in several Latin American countries. Thus, in Nicaragua in 1979, the Sandinista revolutionaries ended the dictatorship of the Somoza family, which had held power since 1936, and set up a regime aligned with Cuba and the USSR.

Dictatorships: Chile and Argentina

In many Latin American countries (Peru, Bolivia, Brazil), military juntas seized power in the 1970s. In Chile, the socialist Salvador Allende was elected president in 1970 and began reforms, including nationalization of the copper mines owned by American interests. In 1973, a coup d'état brought General Pinochet to power. He set up a dictatorship: Allende was assassinated, political parties were banned and hundreds of political opponents were executed. In Argentina, Juan Perón was president beginning in 1946. Relying on the poorest sections of society and the trade unions, and supported by the Argentine people, he promised more social justice and confiscated property of companies belonging to U.S. citizens. His actions aroused opposition from powerful landowners, the Church and the army. In 1955, he was overthrown by a military coup. He returned to power in 1973, but the military under General Videla took control again in 1976 and instituted a reign of terror: thousands of political opponents (the "disappeared") were carried off and secretly executed.

The return of democracy

In the 1980s, the military regimes gradually collapsed. In 1982, Argentina went to war with Britain over the Falkland Islands and lost. The mothers of the disappeared held silent demonstrations every week in the Plaza de Mayo in Buenos Aires. International opinion was mobilized against the regime. In 1982, the generals were overthrown and democracy was restored under the new president, Raul Alfonsín. In Chile, Pinochet gave up the presidency, and democracy was reestablished in 1990. In Brazil, where the military had been in power since the 1960s,

Carnival in Salvador de Bahia in Brazil.

elections with universal suffrage were held for the first time and José Sarney became president.

Determination to expand

Since 1980, the Latin American countries have had major economic difficulties. To build factories and develop agriculture, they borrowed enormous sums of money and were forced to restrict their spending to repay foreign debts. As part of their effort to break away from the political and economic influence of the United States, which has intervened directly in some states (Colombia, Haiti and Panama, for instance), the region's states affirmed a determination to expand economically. Mexico, for example, has worked to develop its industry since the 1930s. In 1992, it signed the North American Free Trade Agreement (NAFTA) with the United States and Canada. This agreement provides for the lifting of tariffs by the three countries to create a sizable single market. Elsewhere, other Latin American countries have formed customs unions to help them meet the challenge of North American competition. □

Signature in 1992 of the free trade agreement between Mexico, Canada and the United States.

Peru

Peru, on the west coast of South America, has experienced many years of military dictatorships and coups d'état. In 1980, democracy was restored. In 1990, Alberto Fujimori (below) became president; he is a descendant of Japanese immigrants. ▼

Fidel Castro

Committed to the struggle against President Batista from 1952, imprisoned and then exiled to Mexico, Fidel Castro landed in Cuba in 1956 and organized a guerrilla army that took power in 1959. He is pictured (opposite) entering the island's capital, Havana, in triumph. Prime minister and, from 1976, Cuba's head of state, Castro was increasingly isolated after the fall of the communist regimes of the USSR and Eastern Europe, which had backed him economically.

Little by little, the countries of western Europe have created the European Union. Countries in eastern Europe freed themselves from the influence of the USSR, and the USSR itself broke up into 15 independent states.

Europe: Western

- **1953** USSR: death of Stalin.
- **1956** Hungary: uprising against Soviet domination.
- **1957** Creation of the EEC (six members).
- **1968** Czechoslovakia: reform movement or "Prague spring."
- **1974** Portugal: "revolution of the carnations." Greece: end of the military dictatorship.
- **1975** Spain: death of Franco.
- **1985** USSR: Gorbachev in power.
- **1989** Germany: removal of the Berlin wall.
- **1991** Breakup of the USSR into independent states.
- **1992** Treaty of Maastricht: creation of the European Union.
- **1995** The European Union includes fifteen member states.

After the reconstruction of economies ruined by the Second World War, most of the countries of Western Europe experienced a period of growth for nearly thirty years. Political and economic life has been characterized by the gradual construction of a united Europe.

The growth years

After 1945, the western European countries rebuilt their economies. From 1950 to the beginning of the 1970s, populations increased, technological progress was rapid, and there seemed to be no limit to potential growth. At the same time, the western European countries worked toward closer links and cooperation. In 1957, the German Federal Republic (GFR), France, Italy, the Netherlands, Belgium and Luxembourg signed the Treaty of Rome, which created the European Economic Community (EEC), or Common Market. Its object was to set up a large market without frontiers in which people, goods and money circulate freely. In 1973, the EEC expanded to include Denmark, Ireland and the United Kingdom.

Political developments

In the 1950s, the three major European powers were the United Kingdom, France and the German Federal Republic (West Germany). From 1958, France was governed by General de Gaulle, who dominated French politics for more than ten years and established the Fifth Republic, which is still in force. The GFR was created in 1949 and led until 1963 by Chancellor Konrad Adenauer, who was active in the formation of the EEC. Under his government, the West German economy made a spectacular recovery, and the country became a major economic power. Britain, governed in turn by the Labour party and the Conservatives,

The European Parliament building in Strasbourg. ▼

Representatives of the EEC states at the Birmingham summit in 1992.

Europe

Campaign during the referendum in Denmark on ratification of the Treaty of Maastricht (1992).

went through a more difficult period and never regained the first-ranking position that it had held before the war. In the rest of the western Europe, three dictatorships became democracies. In 1974, the people of Portugal showered with flowers soldiers who refused to continue fighting in the African colonies: this "revolution of the carnations" overthrew the dictatorship of Salazar, which had lasted since 1926. In Greece, the dictatorial rule of the military junta set up in 1967 ended in 1974, and basic freedoms were restored. In Spain, after the death of Franco in 1975, King Juan Carlos also restored democracy. Since then, all the western European states have been democracies, whether republics like France, Germany, Ireland and Italy or monarchies like Britain, Belgium, Sweden and the Netherlands.

Toward the European Union

After a period of thirty years' rapid growth, Europe went through a difficult period beginning in the 1960s. At the end of that decade, protest movements broke out in several countries. In 1968, student movements led to riots in France, and also in Italy and in Germany. From 1973, Europe was affected by the Middle East oil crisis (see p. 107). Economic conditions changed: production increased more slowly, currencies lost value and companies laid off workers. No government had much success in solving these problems. From 1979, Britain's prime minister was Margaret Thatcher, a Conservative. Her government followed a policy of "privatization"—returning state-run utilities (gas, electricity, etc.) to the private sector, strict control of the money supply and curbing the powers of trade unions. In France, the socialist François Mitterand became president in 1981; his government instituted economic and social reforms. Mitterand and Helmut Kohl, head of the West German government from 1982, played a key role in the development of the EEC. The EEC accepted Greece in 1981, and Spain and Portugal in 1986. In 1992, the Treaty of Maastricht created the European Union: in particular it provided for a single currency and laid the bases for political union. In 1995, Sweden, Finland and Austria joined the European Community, which is today one of the great world economic powers. Other states, notably Turkey and the newly democratic states of eastern Europe, have applied to join. □

The beginnings of the EEC

The European Economic Community (EEC) was formed after the Second World War, thanks largely due to the efforts of its French planners Robert Schuman (above) and Jean Monnet (below, visiting a steel factory). Both wanted Germany to be integrated in an economically strong Europe. The first step was the creation in 1951 of the European Coal and Steel Community (ECSC) among France, the GFR, Italy, the Netherlands, Belgium and Luxembourg. In 1957, these six states signed the Treaty of Rome that founded the EEC.

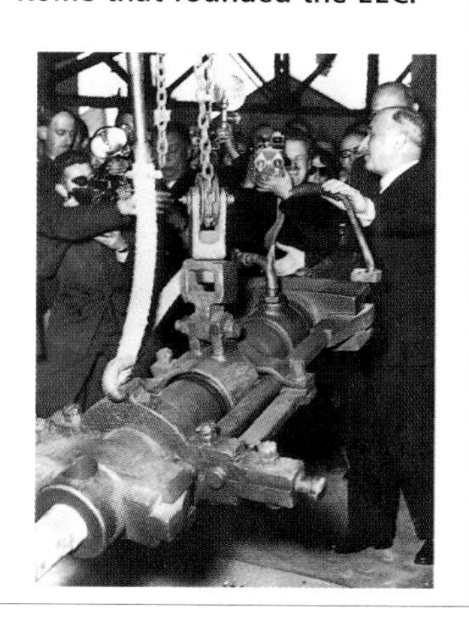

Lech Walesa speaking at a meeting of Solidarity.

Eastern Europe

The Hungarian uprising

In November 1956, the Hungarians rose up against Soviet domination. To repress the revolt, the USSR sent tanks into Budapest. Despite their resistance, the rebels were crushed and the head of the Hungarian government, Imre Nagy, was hanged.

Leonid Brezhnev

Leonid Brezhnev (on the right) was leader of the USSR from 1964 to 1982. In 1974, he met U.S. president Gerald Ford (on the left) at Vladivostok in Siberia.

After 1945, the USSR wielded influence over the countries it controlled in the eastern bloc (see p. 100-101). At the beginning of the 1990s, the USSR broke up into fifteen independent states, while the former communist states of eastern Europe moved toward democracy.

The USSR and the people's democracies

After the Second World War, the USSR extended its domination over eastern Europe. Authoritarian regimes were set up, governed by communist parties on the Soviet model; these states were known as "people's democracies" but were undemocratic.

Only communist Yugoslavia, led by Tito, rejected Soviet influence. After Stalin's death in 1953, Nikita Khrushchev led the USSR. In 1955, the Warsaw Pact military alliance was created between the USSR, Albania, Bulgaria, Poland, Romania, Hungary, Czechoslovakia and the German Democratic Republic (East Germany). In 1956, Khrushchev denounced Stalin's crimes and set in motion de-Stalinization. Detainees were freed from the prison camps known as gulags, and censorship was eased. However, the USSR maintained its domination over its satellite neighbors. In 1956, Hungary revolted against Soviet rule, but the Red Army bloodily suppressed the rising and put in power a government loyal to Moscow. In 1964, Khrushchev was replaced by Brezhnev. Reform movements took hold in the eastern European countries. In 1968, the

The destruction of the Berlin Wall on 9 November 1989.

Mikhail Gorbachev in Uzbekistan, in 1988.

Czechoslovaks tried to introduce "socialism with a human face" (a movement known as the Prague Spring), but this attempt at reform was crushed by troops of the Warsaw Pact. In Poland, riots in the Gdansk shipyards led to the creation in 1980 of the committee of trade unions *Solidarnosc* (Solidarity), directed by Lech Walesa, who led the struggle against the communist authorities.

The end of communism

After the death of Brezhnev in 1982, the USSR went through a period of transition. On the coming to power in 1985 of Mikhail Gorbachev, the regime began to democratize. This was the period of *glasnost* (openness) and *perestroika* (reconstruction): "private cooperatives" were authorized, meetings between Gorbachev and two U.S. presidents, Reagan and then George Bush, moved disarmament forward. Gradually, the old eastern bloc began to break up. In Poland there were general elections in August 1989, and for the first time a noncommunist prime minister came to power. An important symbolic event took place on 9 November 1989: the destruction of the Berlin Wall, built in 1961 to prevent Germans fleeing from the east to the west. In the following months, communist regimes collapsed one after the other. In Czechoslovakia, an opponent of the communists, Vaclav Havel, was elected president. In Romania, Nicolae Ceausescu was overthrown by a violent uprising. Democratic governments were set up in Hungary, Poland and Czechoslovakia. Germany was reunited. The Baltic republics of Lithuania, Latvia and Estonia achieved their independence from the USSR in 1991. The Soviet Union was dissolved and Mikhail Gorbachev resigned.

Eastern Europe today

After the breakup of the USSR, independent states corresponding to the former Soviet republics were formed. Twelve of these joined together in an organization called the Commonwealth of Independent States (CIS). These states, the largest and most powerful of which is Russia, have severe economic and social difficulties. Dissension between different peoples within the same state has caused conflicts; for example, the war between Armenia and Azerbaijan, and the attempted secession of the Chechens from Russia. Similar problems have caused still more serious violence in former Yugoslavia. From 1991, this central European country was torn apart by a civil war. By contrast, the Slovaks and Czechs separated peacefully in Czechoslovakia, where in 1993 two states were created: the Czech Republic and Slovakia.

Yugoslavia ▲

Yugoslavia was made up of several republics until it broke up in 1991. Sarajevo, which was under siege for nearly four years, became the symbol of the war that tore Yugoslavia apart.

Vaclav Havel

In 1989, this Czech writer became the first postwar democratically elected president of Czechoslovakia. In 1992, he became president of the Czech Republic. ▼

UNTAG
NAMIBIA

The United Nations

These Namibian children are waving signs written in Afrikaans in support of the United Nations. The UN was created in 1945 to safeguard international peace and security after the end of the Second World War. In 1948, it adopted the Universal Declaration of Human Rights, which includes the right of peoples to self-determination—that is, to decide if they want to be independent. The UN acted in Namibia's favor to help it become independent from South Africa in 1990. Above, sacks of rice sent by the UN to Somalia.

	Europe	Asia
−3000		**Sumer:** Invention of writing.
−2500	**Western Europe:** Bronze Age.	**India:** Cities of the Indus civilization. **Mesopotamia:** Sargon king of Akkad (2300).
−2000	**Crete:** Minoan era.	**Mesopotamia:** Hammurabi publishes the first code of laws. **India:** Aryan invasions; first sacred books of Hinduism. **China:** Shang dynasty (1800?-1025?).
−1500	**Greece:** Dark Ages (1200-900).	**China:** Zhou dynasty (1025-256).
−1000	**Greece:** First city-states (850), colonization of the Mediterranean (700-500). **Rome:** Founding of Rome (753), founding of the republic (509).	**Palestine:** David king of Israel. **Mesopotamia:** Nebuchadnezzar king of Babylonia (605-562). **India:** Life of Siddhartha Gautama the Buddha (560?–480?). **China:** Life of Confucius (551-479).
−500	**Greece:** Persian Wars (490-479); reign of Alexander the Great (336-323).	**Asia Minor, Iran:** Conquests by Alexander (333-327). **India:** Reign of Asoka (269?–232). **China:** The Qin dynasty founds the empire (221).
−200	**Greece:** Greece becomes a Roman province (146). **Rome:** End of the republic and beginning of the empire (27).	**China:** Han dynasty.
1	**Rome:** Julio-Claudian dynasty (to 68), Flavian dynasty (to 96), Antonine dynasty (to 192), Severian dynasty (to 235).	**India:** Kushan empire (first and second centuries). **Palestine:** Death of Jesus (33?).
200	**Rome:** Division into Western and Eastern Empires (395). Fall of the Western Empire (476).	**China:** End of the Han dynasty (220). **Iran:** Sassanid dynasty (224-651).
500	**Byzantine Empire:** Reign of Justinian (527-565). **Western Europe:** Rise of barbarian kingdoms.	**China:** Arrival of Buddhism.
600		**China:** Tang dynasty (618-907). **Arabia:** Beginnings of Islam (622). **Syria, Palestine:** Muslim conquest (600s–700s).
700	**Spain:** Muslim conquest.	**Japan:** Nara (710-794), then Heian-kyo (794-1185), capitals of the empire.
800	**Western Europe:** Charlemagne crowned emperor (800), division of the empire (843). Norman invasions.	**Cambodia:** First building at Angkor.
900	**Western Europe:** Birth of the Holy Roman Empire in Germany (962). Capetian dynasty in France (987).	**China:** Song dynasty (960-1279). **Japan:** Beginning of clan warfare (around 940).
1000	**Byzantine Empire:** Separation of the Orthodox and Latin churches (1054). **Western Europe:** Norman Conquest of England (1066).	**Syria, Palestine:** First Crusade (1096-1099). **Vietnam:** Ly dynasty unifies the country (1010-1225).
1100		**Japan:** Beginning of the rule of the shoguns (1192).
1200	**Byzantine Empire:** Crusaders take Constantinople (1204). Reconquest of Constantinople by the Byzantines (1261).	**Central Asia:** Beginnings of Mongol expansion. **China:** Yuan dynasty, founded by the Mongols (1279-1368).
1300	**Western Europe:** Hundred Years' War between France and England (1337-1453). The Black Death (1347-1353).	**Japan:** The Ashikaga family rises to power (1333-1573). **China:** Ming dynasty (1368-1664).
1400	**Byzantine Empire:** Constantinople falls to the Turks (1453). **Western Europe:** The Spanish take Grenada from the Muslims, ending the Reconquista (1492).	**Japan:** Civil war (1467-1477).
1500	**Europe:** Protestant Reformation. Catholic Counter-Reformation. **Holy Roman Empire:** Reign of Charles V (1519-1556).	**India:** Babur (1494-1530), founder of the Mogul Empire. **Turkey:** Reign of Suleiman the Magnificent (1520-1566).

AFRICA	THE AMERICAS/OCEANIA	
Egypt: Old Kingdom (2660-2180). First hieroglyphs.	**Central America:** Domestication of maize.	−3000
Egypt: Middle Kingdom (2060-1650).		−2500
Sahara: Wall paintings in Tasili Plateau (modern Algeria).	**Central America:** First villages in Oaxaca.	−2000
Egypt: New Kingdom (1530-1069).	**Mexico:** Olmec civilization (1000-400).	−1500
North Africa: Carthage founded (814). **Egypt:** Late Period (after 664).	**Andes Mountains:** Chavín era (800s–200s).	−1000
Egypt: Conquest by Alexander (332); Greek influence. **Carthage:** Punic Wars with Rome.	**Oceania:** Settlement of the Marquesas Islands. **Mexico:** Zapotec civilization (from 500 BC to about AD 750).	−500
Egypt: Battle of Actium (31). Egypt becomes a Roman province.		−200
	Peru: Rise of Moche culture (100s–700s).	1
	Central America: Height of Mayan civilization (200s–900s). **Peru:** Beginnings of Nazca civilization (200s–600s).	200
	Oceania: Settlement of Hawaii (between 300 and 500).	500
Egypt, North Africa: Muslim conquest.		600
	North America: Mound Builders in Ohio and Mississippi valleys.	700
	Oceania: Except for New Guinea, all islands populated.	800
Egypt, North Africa: Fatimid dynasty (909–1171).	**North America:** Vikings discover Greenland (982).	900
Subsaharan Africa: Ife civilization in Nigeria. Founding of the empire of Mali. **North Africa:** Expansion of the Almoravids.	**North America:** Anasazi build Mesa Verde (modern Colorado). Settlement of the Iroquois and Hurons in Canada. Viking expeditions.	1000
North Africa: Almohad dynasty (1130-1269).	**Andes Mountains:** Expansion of the Chimù Empire.	1100
Subsaharan Africa: Expansion of the empire of Mali.	**Andes Mountains:** The Incas found Cuzco.	1200
Subsaharan Africa: Height of the kingdom of Great Zimbabwe.	**North America:** Apache and Navajo civilization. **Central America:** The Aztecs found Tenochtitlán (1325).	1300
Subsaharan Africa: Kingdom of Monomotapa. Portuguese exploration (after 1430).	**Central America:** Christopher Columbus reaches the Antilles (1492) and later the American mainland.	1400
Egypt, North Africa: Conquest by the Ottoman Turks (1517-1587).	**South America:** Pedro Cabral discovers Brazil (1500).	1500

	Europe	Asia
1550	**The Netherlands:** Birth of the United Provinces (1581). **France:** Wars of Religion (1562-1598).	**India:** Reign of Akbar (1556-1605). **China:** The Portuguese establish a trading post at Macao (1557).
1600	**England:** Execution of Charles I (1649). Oliver Cromwell in power (1649-1658).	**Japan:** Tokugawa shoguns rule from Edo (Tokyo) (1603). **China:** End of the Ming dynasty (1644). Qing dynasty (1644-19
1650	**France:** Reign of Louis XIV, the Sun King (1643-1715). **Russia:** Reign of Peter the Great (1682-1725).	**India:** Reign of Aurangzeb (1658-1707). **China:** Reign of Kangxi (1662-1722).
1700	**Austria:** Reign of Empress Maria Theresa (1740-1780). **Russia:** Reign of Frederick the Great (1740-1786).	
1750	**Russia:** Reign of Catherine II, the Great (1762-1796). **France:** French Revolution (1789-1799).	**India:** Beginning of English colonization (1773).
1800	**Europe:** Conquests by Emperor Napoleon I (to 1815). National uprisings (1830, 1848). **Great Britain:** The first labor unions. Queen Victoria (1837-1901). **Austria:** Reign of Francis Joseph (1848-1916).	**China:** Opium Wars (1840-1842). English victory.
1850	**Italy:** Unification of kingdom of Italy (1861). **Germany:** Proclamation of the German Empire (1871).	**India:** Sepoy Rebellion against the British (1857-1859). **Indochina:** French colonization. **Japan:** Beginning of the Meiji era, reforms (1867).
1900	**Russia:** First Russian Revolution (1905). **Europe:** Founding of the Triple Entente (France, Great Britain and Russia) against Germany (1907).	**China:** Boxer Rebellion (1900). **Japan:** Japanese victory in the Russo-Japanese War (1905).
1910	**Central Europe:** Balkan wars (1910-1913). **Europe:** World War I (1914-1918). **Russia:** Russian Revolution (1917) brings Lenin to power.	**China:** End of the Qing dynasty, proclamation of the republic (**Japan:** Enters World War I (1914). **Middle East:** Homeland f Jews created in Palestine with Balfour Declaration (1917).
1920	**Russia:** Creation of the USSR (1922), Stalin takes power (1924). **Italy:** Mussolini and fascists come to power (1922).	**Turkey:** Mustafa Kemal creates the Turkish republic (1923). **China:** Chiang Kai-shek comes to power (1927).
1930	**Germany:** Adolf Hitler assumes power (1933). **Spain:** Civil war (1936-1939); Francisco Franco in power. **France:** Popular Front government (1936). **Europe:** Start of World War II (1939).	**India:** Mohandas Gandhi leads the March to the Sea protesting on salt (1930). **China:** Japanese invade Manchuria (1931). Lon March by the communists (1934-1936). **Japan:** Occupation northeastern China (1937).
1940	**Europe:** German successes (to 1943) followed by Allied victories (1943-1945); end of World War II (1945). **Great Britain:** Churchill prime minister (1940-1945, 1951-1955). **Germany:** Division into East and West Germany (1949).	**Japan:** World War II. Atomic bombs dropped on Hiroshima ar Nagasaki (1945). **India:** Independence from Great Britain (19 **Middle East:** Proclamation of the State of Israel (1948). **China:** People's Republic, Mao Zedong in power (1949).
1950	**Europe:** Treaty of Rome: six nations found European Economic Community (EEC) (1957). **Hungary:** Soviet tanks put down uprising (1956). **USSR:** Khrushchev in power (1956-1964). **France:** Charles de Gaulle founds the Fifth Republic (1958).	**Indonesia:** Independent since 1949, hosts Bandung Conference non-aligned countries (1955). **Southeast Asia:** Independence countries of French Indochina (1953-1954), Vietnam War (1954-1975). **Korea:** Korean War (1950-1953).
1960	**Germany:** Building of the Berlin Wall (1961). **Czechoslovakia:** Soviet intervention ends reforms (1968).	**Middle East:** Six Day War between Israel and Arab nations (1967).
1970	**Europe:** The EEC expands to nine member states (1973). **Greece:** Fall of the military regime (1974). **Portugal:** Revolution of the Carnations overthrows dictatorship (1974). **Spain:** Death of Franco, end of dictatorship (1975).	**China:** Death of Mao Zedong, Deng Xiaoping assumes power. **Middle East:** Yom Kippur War between Israel and Arab nations Civil war in Lebanon (1975-1982). **Iran:** Islamic revolution b Ayatollah Khomeini to power (1979).
1980	**USSR:** Mikhail Gorbachev comes to power (1985). **Germany:** Fall of the Berlin Wall (1989).	**Cambodia:** Khmer Rouge regime devastates the country. **China:** Repression of pro-democracy demonstrations in Beijing
1990	**USSR:** Soviet Union dissolved (1991). **Yugoslavia:** Dissolution. Wars in Slovenia, Croatia, Bosnia, Kosovo (Serbia). **Russia:** Yeltsin, first democratic president.	**Middle East:** Peace agreements between Israel and the PLO (19 **Indonesia:** President Suharto resigns (1999).

Africa	The Americas/Oceania	Year
Subsaharan Africa: Moroccans conquer the Songhai Empire (1591).	**North America:** First unsuccessful attempt at colonization by the English (modern North Carolina) (1584).	**1550**
	North America: First English settlement at Jamestown, VA (1607), Plymouth, MA (1620). Champlain explores Canada.	**1600**
South Africa: Cape Town founded by the Dutch (1652).	**North America:** New York founded by the Dutch as New Amsterdam (1664).	**1650**
	Oceania: Discovery of Easter Island (1722).	**1700**
Subsaharan Africa: Ashanti civilization (modern Ghana).	**North America:** The English conquer Canada (1763). Declaration of Independence by the United States (1776).	**1750**
Subsaharan Africa: Peul empire of Sokoto (modern Nigeria) (1804-1844). Slave trade abolished by England (1807), France (1815). **North Africa:** Algeria conquered by France (1830).	**South America:** Independence of Venezuela, Argentina, Chile, Colombia, Peru, Mexico and Brazil. **North America:** Settlement of the western United States.	**1800**
Egypt: Construction of the Suez Canal (1859-1869). **Subsaharan Africa:** Berlin Conference on central Africa and the Congo (1884-1885). **South Africa:** Boer War (1899-1902).	**North America:** Civil War (1861-1865), Indian wars. **Canada:** Creation of the Canadian Confederation (1867).	**1850**
		1900
North Africa: French protectorate over Morocco (1912). **Subsaharan Africa:** Colonies participate in World War I.	**Central America:** Mexican Revolution (1911). Panama Canal opens (1912). **United States:** Entry into World War I against Germany (1917).	**1910**
	United States: Great Depression begins with stock market crash (1929).	**1920**
Ethiopia: Beginning of the reign of Emperor Haile Selassie (1930-1974).	**South America:** Dictatorships in Brazil and Argentina. **North America, Oceania:** Independence for Canada, Australia and New Zealand with the Statute of Westminster (1931). **United States:** Roosevelt elected president (1932) New Deal.	**1930**
North Africa: World War II. Allied landings in Morocco, Algeria, and Tunisia.	**United States:** American entry into World War II after the Japanese attack on Pearl Harbor (1941). **Argentina:** Perón regime (1946-1955).	**1940**
North Africa: Algerian war of independence (1954-1962). Morocco and Tunisia independent (1956). **Subsaharan Africa:** Ghana is first of British colonies to become independent (1957).	**United States:** Harry S Truman (1945-1953), Dwight D. Eisenhower (1953-1960) elected president. Martin Luther King leads the civil-rights stuggle (1955-1968). **Cuba:** Fidel Castro comes to power (1959).	**1950**
Subsaharan Africa: Independence for Congo (from Belgium), French colonies, and Nigeria (from Great Britain) (1960).	**United States:** John F. Kennedy, elected president in 1961, assassinated (1963).	**1960**
Subsaharan Africa: Angola and Mozambique gain independence from Portugal (1975).	**South America:** Government overthrown by military in Chile (1973). Dictatorships in Brazil (1964-1985) and Argentina (1976-1983). Fall of the Somoza dictatorship in Nicaragua (1979).	**1970**
South Africa: Namibia becomes independent (1989).	**United States:** Ronald Reagan president (1981-1989).	**1980**
South Africa: End of apartheid (racial segregation) (1991). **North Africa:** Rise of Islamic fundamentalism.	**United States:** Americans intervene in the Gulf War (1991).	**1990**

Index

Note: An entry in **bold type** indicates that an illustration accompanies the text.

Photo Credits

Couverture : gh Calamon I./Stock Image, Paris : *Armée enterrée de Qin* – **gm** Dagli Orti G., *Château de Versailles : Louis XIV entouré de Louvois, Mansart et Lenôtre vers 1690* – **gb** Held S., *Nawallgar : Peinture murale* (XIXe s.) – **mb** Studio Koppermann, *Glyptothek, Munich : Guerrier grec mourant* – **h** Nogues A./Sygma : *Chute du mur de Berlin (1989)*

Dos Dagli Orti G. : *Laboureur égyptien (Thèbes)*

Gardes : Lessing E./Magnum, *Musée de l'Homme, Paris : Peinture rupestre du Tassili*

Page titre : Riboud M./Magnum : *Jeunes pionniers pendant la Révolution culturelle* –

2-hg Bibliothèque nationale de France, Paris : *Paiement des redevances (Miniature)* – **2-b** Keystone : *Impératrice Nagako (épouse d'Hiro Hito)* – **3-h** Dagli Orti G, *Musée du Louvre, Paris : Stèle des vautours, détail des soldats (2450 av. J.C.)* – **4-hg** Dagli Orti G., *Musée de Turin* – **4-hm** Dagli Orti G., *Musée national, Copenhague* – **4-hd** Dagli Orti G, *Musée de la Marine, Paris* – **4-mhg** De Cox/Fotogram-Stone – **4-mgm** Travert Y./Diaf – **4-mgb** Dagli Orti G., *Musée archéologique, Naples* – **4-mdh** Josse H., *Bibliothèque nationale de France* – **4-mdm** Bibliothèque nationale de France, Paris – **4-bg** Comissao national para as comemoraçaoes, Lisbonne : *Caravelle Santa Maria de Christophe Colomb* – **4-bd** Dagli Orti G., *Bibliothèque publique et universitaire, Sienne* – **5-hg** AKG, Paris – **5-mgh** Dagli Orti G., *Musée d'art moderne, Milan* – **5-bg** Durazzo M./ANA – **5-hd** Bossu R./Sygma – **5-hm** Norcia Mike/Sygma – **5-mdh** – **5-mdm** Dieter/Gamma – **5-mdb** B et F. prod/Pix – **5-bd** Apesteguy F./Gamma – **6-hg** Westlight-Zuckerman J./Cosmos – **6-h** Lessing E./Magnum, *Musée de l'Homme, Paris : Serviteurs crétois (Réplique du palais de Cnossos)* – **6-mh** Dagli Orti G., *Musée de Turin* – **6-mb** De Cox/Fotogram-Stone – **6-b** Dagli Orti G., *Musée archéologique, Naples* – **7-h** Dagli Orti G., *Musée du Louvres, Paris : Relief du palais de Sargon, Khorsabad* – **7-b** Held S. : *Détail du stupa de Sanchi* – **8-hg** Lessing E./Magnum, *Musée national, Budapest : Trois urnes anthropomorphiques (Néolithique)* – **8-bg** Dagli Orti G., *Musée Boucher de Perthes, Abbeville* – **8-d** Réunion des Musées nationaux, Paris, *Musée des antiquités nationales, St-Germain-en-Laye* – **9-h** Lessing E./Magnum, *Musée de l'Homme, Paris* – **9-mg** Dagli Orti G., *Musée des antiquités nationales, St-Germain-en-Laye* – **9-hd** AKG, Paris – **9-b** Lessing E./Magnum, *Musée Narony, Belgrade* – **10-h** Dagli Orti G., *Musée du Louvre, Paris : Tablette économique summérienne (prov. Tello)* – **10-bg** Dagli Orti G., *Musée du Louvre, Paris* – **11-h** Percheron R./Artephot, *British Museum, Londres* – **11-m** Lessing E./Magnum, *British Museum, Londres* – **11-b** Lessing E./Magnum, *Musée du Louvre, Paris* – **12-h** Dagli Orti G., *Musée égyptien, Le Caire : Scribe égyptien* – **12-m** Dagli Orti G., *Thèbes* – **12-b** Dagli Orti G., *Musée du Louvre, Paris* – **13-h** Dagli Orti G., *Musée égyptien, Turin : Détail du sarcophage de Diethotefanch* – **13-md** Bildarchiv Preussischer Kulturbesitz – **13-bg** Nimatallah/Artephot, *Musée égyptien, Turin* – **13-bd** AKG, Paris, *Musée égyptien, Berlin* – **14-h** Dagli Orti G., *Ceylan : Sculpture d'un cuisinier (époque Han)* – **14-m** Dagli Orti G., *Musée national, Karachi* – **15-h** Held S. – **15-m** Ravaux M./Réunion des Musées nationaux, Paris, *Musée Guimet, Paris* – **15-b** Held S. – **16-h** Dagli Orti G., *Musée Cernuschi, Paris* – **16-m** Dagli Orti G., *Musée Cernuschi, Paris* – **17-h** De Cox/Fotogram-Stone – **17-m** Stierlin H., *Musée de Tokyo* – **17-b** Belzeaux/Rapho – **18/19** Calamon I./Stock Image, Paris – **19-h** Dagli Orti G., *Musée Cernuschi, Paris* – **20-h** Stierlin H., *Musée d'Athènes : Masque dit d'Agamemnon* – **20b** Ruiz H./Hoa-Qui, *Palais de Cnossos : Fresque du roi-prêtre* – **21-h** Travert Y./Diaf – **21-m** Nimatallah/Artephot, *Villa Giulia, Rome* – **21-b** Dagli Orti G., *Musée d'art grec, Chatillon-sur-Seine* – **22-h** Dagli Orti G., *Musée archéologique, Naples* – **22-mg** Dagli Orti G., *Musée archéologique, Naples* – **22-b** Studio Koppermann, *Glyptothek, Munich* – **23-h** Dagli Orti G., *Musée archéologique, Naples* – **23-m** Dagli Orti G., *Musée National, Athènes* – **23-b** Dagli Orti G., *Musée du Louvre* – **24-h** Scala, *Musée civique, Plaisance : Portrait d'un Républicain* – **24-b** Dagli Orti G., *Musée du Capitole, Rome* – **25-h** Dagli Orti G., *Musée archéologique, Naples : Fresque provenant de Paestum* – **25-g** Dagli Orti G., *Musée du Capitole, Rome* – **25-d** Dagli Orti G., *Musée national, Carthage* – **26-h** Dagli Orti G., *Musée national des Thermes, Rome* – **26-m** AKG, *Paris, Villa romaine de Nennig, Allemagne : Mosaïque, IIe s. apr. J.-C.* – **26-b** Dagli Orti G., *Musée national des Thermes, Rome* – **26-g** Badisches Landesmuseum, Karlsruhe – **27-h** Dagli Orti G., *Musée archéologique, Naples* – **27-b** Held S. – **28-hg** Held A./Artephot, *Musée d'Ifé, Nigeria : Couple, art d'Ifé* – **28-h** Dagli Orti G., *Ravenne* – **28-mh** Dagli Orti G., *Palais public, Sienne* – **28-mb** Dagli Orti G. – **28-b** Dagli Orti G., *Musée national d'archéologie, Lima* – **29-h** Michaud R. et S./Rapho, *Musée de Topkapi, Istanbul : Cavalier turco-mongol (Miniature du XVe s.)* – **29-b** Coll. Larousse, *Bibliothèque nationale de France, Paris : Jeanne d'Arc conduite près de Charles VII* – **30-h** Coll. Larousse, *Bibliothèque nationale de France, Paris : Prise de Constantinople par les Turcs* – **30-m** AKG, Paris, *Bibliothèque nationale d'Espagne, Madrid* – **30-b** Dagli Orti G. : *Mosaïque byzantine, église San Vital (Ravenne, VIe s.)* – **31-h** Dagli Orti G. : *Mosaïque byzantine, église San Vital (Ravenne, VIe s.)* – **31-m** Thierry N. – **31-b** Coll. Larousse, *Bibliothèque nationale de France, Paris : Miniature du extraite de « Voyage en terre d'outre-mer » (1455)* – **32-h** Josse H., *Bibliothèque nationale de France, Paris : Harun al Rachid de Kamal al-din Behzad (766-809)* – **32-m** Cristofori M./Ask Images – **32-b** Mandel G./Artephot, *Musée de Topkapi, Istanbul : Miniature turcque représentant la bataille de Badr* – **33-h** Bibliothèque nationale de France, Paris – **33-m** Collection E.S./Explorer – **33-b** Bibliothèque nationale de France, Paris : Miniature extraite des Maqâmât d'al-Hariri – **34-h** Bibliothèque nationale de France, Paris – **34-m** Bibliothèque nationale de France, Paris : *Miniature arabe du XIIIe s. (1237), École de Bagdad* – **34-b** Bibliothèque nationale de France, Paris : *Extrait du « Livre des Rois » de Firdoussi (1546)* – **35-h** Josse H., *Bibliothèque nationale de France, Paris : Miniature persane extraite de « Jami al-Tawârîkh » (XVIe s.)* – **35-b** Degeorge G. – **35-m** D.R., *Musée de Topkapi, Istanbul* – **36-h** Nimatallah/Artephot, *Musée d'art historique, Vienne : Couronne de Charlemagne ou du Saint Empire romain (1050)* – **36-m** Edimedia, *British Museum : Miniature extraite de « Sancti beati de liebana explanatione apocalypsine » (1109)* – **36-b** Chirol S. – **37-h** Dagli Orti G., *Trésor de la cathédrale, Bayeux : Tapisserie dite de la reine Mathilde* – **37-m** Dagli Orti G., *Musée Goya, Castres : Miniature extraite de « Les grandes chroniques de France », École du Nord (XIVe s.)* – **37-bd** Gaillarde R./Gamma – **37-hd** Gaillarde R./Gamma – **38-h** Chirol S. – **38-mg** Varga/Artephot, *Bibliothèque Ste-Geneviève* – **38-md** Degeorge G. – **38-bg** Bibliothèque nationale de France, Paris : *Miniature extraite de « La destruction de Troie » de Benoît de Ste-More (XIVe s.)* – **38-bd** Scala, *Bargello, Florence* – **39-h** Dagli Orti G., *Musée national, Copenhague* – **39-b** Bibliothèque nationale de France, Paris : *Miniature extraite des « Heures de Charles d'Angoulême » (v. 1480)* – **40-h** Dagli Orti G., *Palais public, Sienne : Fresque allégorique de la Salle de la Paix* – **40-m** British Museum, Londres – **40-b** Bibliothèque nationale de France, Paris – **41-h** Bibliothèque nationale de France, Paris – **41-m** Goldner/Edimages – **41-b** Held A./Artephot, *Bibliothèque de l'Université, Heidelberg : Manuscrit Codex Manesse* – **41-bd** Bayerische Staatsbibliothek, Munich – **42/43** Josse H., *Bibliothèque de l'Arsenal, Paris* – **43-h** Coll. Larousse, *Bibliothèque nationale de France, Paris : Christine de Pisan, Cité des Dames (Miniature)* – **44-h** Bibliothèque nationale de France, Paris : *Kubilay Khan (Manuscrit chinois, 1238)* – **44-m** Réunion des Musées nationaux, Paris, *Musée Guimet* – **45-h** Dagli Orti G. : *Scène extraite du rouleau du Gengi Monotagari (XIIe s.)* – **45-m** Held S. – **45-b** Josse H./Agence des affaires culturelles du Japon – **46-h** Held A./Artephot, *Musée d'Ifé, Nigeria : Tête Ifé en laiton* – **46-b** Bibliothèque nationale de France, Paris : *Miniature extraite des Maqâmât d'al-Hariri* – **47-h** Degeorge G. – **47-mg** Henneghien/ANA – **47-md** Castro F./ANA : *Fresque Lalibela* – **47-b** Held A./ Artephot, *Musée d'Ifé, Nigeria* – **48-h** Darbois/Edimages : *Masque en bois de caribou (art inuit)* – **48-m** Gohier F./Explorer – **48-b** Marco/Ask Images – **49-h** Dagli Orti G., *Musée national d'archéologie, Lima* – **49-bg** Dagli Orti G., *Musée de l'or, Lima* – **49-bd** Bibliothèque nationale de France, Paris : *Scène extraite du Codex Ixtlixochitl (XVIIe s.)* – **50-hg** Dagli Orti G., *Chapelle du Palais Medicis Ricardi, Florence* : Laurent le Magnifique (Fresque de Gozzoli) – **50-h** Josse H., *Musée du Château, Versailles* – **50-mh** Dagli Orti G., *Château de Malmaison* – **50-mb** AKG, Paris, *Musée de la coopération franco-américaine, Blérencourt* – **50-b** Nimatallah/Artephot, *National Maritime Museum, Londres* – **51-h** Dagli Orti G., *Musée Carnavalet, Paris : Départ du citoyen (1792)* – **51-b** Dagli Orti G., *Musée d'art ancien, Lisbonne : Marchands portugais* – **52-h** Dagli Orti G., *Musée naval, Lisbonne : Portrait de Christophe Colomb* – **52-m** Comissao national para as comemoraçaoes, Lisbonne – **52/53** E.T. Archive : *Gravure de Théodore de Bry* – **53-h** Josse H., *Musée de Versailles : Peinture de Théodore Gudin (XIXe s.)* – **53-m** Dagli Orti G., *Villa Farnèse, Caprarola* : Fresque d'A.G. de Varèse (1575) – **53-b** Josse H., *Musée de la ville, St-Malo* – **54-h** E.T. Archive, *Château de Windsor : Henri VIII peint par Holbein (1497-1543)* – **54-b** Scala, *Bargello, Florence* – **55-h** Dagli Orti G., *Bibliothèque publique et universitaire, Sienne : Gravure de Hogenberg (fin XVIe s.)* – **55-mg** AKG, Paris : Gravure de Lucas Cranach – **55-md** Bibliothèque nationale de France, Paris : *Miniature extraite des « Chants royaux sur la conception couronnée du Puy de Rouen » (1519-1528)* – **55-b** Dagli Orti G., *Chapelle du Palais Medicis-Ricardi, Florence : Fresque de Benozzo Gozzoli* – **56-h** Dagli Orti G., *Musée du Château, Versailles : Peinture de J.B. Martin* – **56-b** Josse H, *Musée du Louvre, Paris : Peinture de Adrien van Ostade* – **56-m** Lessing E./Magnum, *Musée d'histoire de la ville de Vienne* – **57-h** Bridgeman Art Library : *Peinture de Sir Anthony van Dick* – **57-m** AKG, Paris, *National Gallery, Londres* – **57-b** AKG, Paris, *Musées royaux d'art et d'histoire, Bruxelles : Peinture de G.A. Berckheyde* – **58-h** Dagli Orti G., *Musée historique, Moscou : L'impératrice Catherine II de Russie peint par F.S. Rokotov (1770)* – **58-b** Lauros/Giraudon, *Château de Sans-Souci, Postdam : Peinture de J.C. Frisch* – **59-h** Dagli Orti G., *Château de Malmaison : « Une soirée chez Madame Joffrin » de A.C. Lemonnier* – **59-m** Dagli Orti G., *Musée historique, Vienne* – **59-b** Josse H., *Bibliothèque nationale de France, Paris* – **60/61** Bridgeman/Giraudon, *National Gallery, Londres* – **61-hd** Tereberine Heifels : *Palais d'été, St-Pétersbourg* – Siny Most – **62-h** The Granger Collection : *The Mayflower (gravure coloriée, 1905)* – **62-b** The Granger Collection : *Lithographie de Curier et Yves (1876)* – **63-h** AKG, Paris, *Musée national de la coopération franco-américaine, Blérencourt* – **63-m** The Granger Collection – **63-bg** The Granger Collection – **63-bd** Lauros/Giraudon, *Bibliothèque nationale de France, Paris* – **64-h** Dagli Orti G., *Bibliothèque des arts décoratifs, Paris : Sans-culotte gardant la famille royale au Temple (gravure de la Révolution française)* – **64-b** Dagli Orti G., *Musée historique lorrain, Nancy* – **65-h** Dagli Orti G., *Musée de la Marine, Paris* – **65-m** Dagli Orti G., *Musée du Château, Versailles : Peinture de P.N. Bergeret* – **65-b** AKG, Paris, *Munich : Peinture d'Engelbert Seibertz* – **66-h** Held S : *Porte du Midi dans la Cité Interdite* – **66-m** Colombel P. – **66/67** Dagli Orti G., *Musée d'art ancien, Lisbonne* – **67-h** Réunion des Musées nationaux, Paris, *Musée Guimet, Paris : Paravent de Namban Byobu dit « des Portugais », École Kano (XVIIe s.)* – **67-m** Held S. – **67-b** Arnaudet D./Réunion des Musées nationaux, Paris, *Musée Guimet, Paris* – **68-h** Dagli Orti G., *Société de Géographie, Paris : Portrait d'un Maori par A. Wahlen (1844)* – **68-m** Dagli Orti G., *Château de Kronborg, Dannemark* – **68-b** Degeorge G. – **69-h** Nimatallah/Artephot, *National Maritime Museum, Londres* – **69-m** Dagli Orti G., *Musée des arts africains et océaniens, Paris* – **69-b** Réunion des Musées nationaux, Paris, *Musée des arts africains et océaniens, Paris* – **70-hg** Layda/Schuster/Explorer : *Statue de la Liberté* – **70-h** Dagli Orti G., *Musée du Louvre, Paris* – **70-mh** Charmet J.L. – **70-mb** Held S. – **70-b** Coll. Larousse, *Musée de l'Armée, Paris* – **71-b** E.T. Archive : *Intérieur du Crystal Palace de Londres (1851)* – **71-h** Charmet J-L./Explorer : *Soldats ashanti* – **72-h** Dagli Orti G., *Musée de l'Ermitage, St-Pétersbourg : Scène de famille au XIXe s. peint par F. M. Slavjanskij (1851)* – **72-m** Jourdes/Edimages – **72/73** Réunion des Musées nationaux, Paris – **73-h** Dagli Orti G., *Musée d'art moderne, Milan : « Les ambassadeurs de la faim » de G. Pelizza da Volpedo* – **73-m** Dagli Orti G., *Musée Karl Marx, Trèves* – **73-bd** Edimedia : *Peinture de Gustave Courbet* – **74-h** Bridgeman Art Library, *Forbes magazine collection, Londres : Peinture de Jennings et Betteridge* – **74-m** Dagli Orti G., *Musée historique de la ville de Vienne* – **74-bg** Josse H., *Musée de Versailles : Peinture de F.X. Winterhalter (1840)* – **74-bd** Dagli Orti G., *Musée historique de la ville de Vienne : Gravure de Hofel (XIXe s.)* – **75-b** Dagli Orti G., *Musée du Risorgimento, Turin : Peinture de G. Induno* – **75-h** AKG, Paris : *Peinture d'Anton von Werner (1885)* – **75-m** Charmet J.L. – **76-h** The Granger Collection, New York : *Sitting Bull (1834-1890) par D.F. Barry* – **76-m** Dagli Orti G., *Musée Bolivar, Caracas : Peinture de Michalena (milieu du XIXe s.)* – **76/77** Cat's/Kipa – **77-h** The Granger Collection, New York : *Lithographie par Kurze et Allison (1886)* – **77-b** The Granger Collection, New York : *Photographie de M. B. Brady (1864)* – **77-bd** Charles/Rapho – **78-h** AKG, Paris : *Impératrice chinoise Tseu Hi (1835-1908) par Hubert Vos (1905)* – **78-b** Abegg W./AKG, Paris – **79-h** Charmet J.L. : *Estampe japonaise (après 1860)* – **79-bd** Roger-Viollet – **79-m** Hulton Deutsch Collection – **80-h** Durazzo M./ANA : *Peinture sur soie du palais d'Udaipur (XVIIIe s.)* – **80-md** Dagli Orti G. : *Gravure du Petit Journal (août 1897)* – **80-mg** Edimedia – **80-b** Macintyre/ANA – **81-h** Held S. – **81-m** Jonas/Kharbine Tapabor – **81-b** L'Illustration/Sygma – **82-h** Charmet J.L./Explorer : *Délimitation des nouvelles frontières franco-allemandes au Congo* – **82-m** Sirot/Tallandier – **82-b** Charmet J.L./Explorer – **83-h** Dagli Orti G., *Musée Condé, Chantilly : Peinture de H. Boulange* – **83-m** Coll. Larousse – **83-bg** Edimedia, *British Museum, Londres : Peinture de G.F. Angus (1847)* – **83-bd** Kharbine Tapabor – **84-h** Dagli Orti G., *Musée de l'Armée, Paris : Soldat allemand avec masque à gaz et cuirasse de guetteur en août 1917 (aquarelle de F. Flameng)* – **84-b** Pia J./Tallandier, *Imperial War Museum, Londres : Aquarelle de H. Chartier (1916)* – **85-h** Coll. Larousse, *Musée de l'Armée, Paris* – **85-m** Coll. Larousse, *Imperial War Museum, Londres* – **85-b** Moreau/Coll. Larousse – **86-hg** Gesgon A./Cirip : *Lénine* – **86-h** Riboud M./Magnum – **86-mh** Willis J./Fotogram-Stone – **86-mb** B et F. prod/Pix – **86-b** Sygma – **87-h** Imperial War Museum, Londres : *Bombardiers anglais* – **87-b** Archive Photos : *Débarquement en Normandie (1944)* – **88-h** Novosti : *Affiche « Tout le pouvoir aux soviets » (1917)* – **88-b** Novosti – **88-m** L'Illustration Sygma – **89-h** Coll. Larousse, *Musée Lénine, Prague* – **89-hd** Harlingue/Roger-Viollet – **89-bd** Roger-Viollet – **89-bg** Novosti – **90-hg** F.P.G./Explorer : *Construction de l'Empire State Building* – **90-m** Coll. Larousse – **90-b** Archives Francis Paudras – **91-h** Edimedia, *Archives SNARK/LC Washington* – **91-md** Keystone – **91-m** Keystone – **91-bd** Keystone – **92-h** Roger-Viollet : *Congés payés (France)* – **92-b** L'Illustration Sygma – **93-h** Associated Press – **93-mg** Tallandier – **93-hd** Keystone – **93-md** Keystone – **93-bd** Roger-Viollet – **93-b** Roger-Viollet – **94-h** Michaud R. et S./Rapho : *Gandhi* – **94-b** L'Illustration Sygma – **95-h** Lipnitzki/Roger-Viollet – **95-m** Hulton Deutsch/Sipa Press – **95-b** L'Illustration Sygma – **96-h** Bildarchiv Preussischer Kulturbesitz : *Chars, Tunisie (1942)* – **96-m** Novosti – **96/97** Archive Photos – **97-h Usis** – DITE – **98-mg** Tallandier – **98-bd** Hulton Deutsch/Sipa Press – **98-h** Roger-Viollet – **99-h** Novosti – **99-b** Keystone – **99-mg** Depardon/Magnum – **99-md** Black Star/Rapho – **100-h** Keystone : Construction du mur de Berlin – **100-m** Keystone – **101-h** Keystone – **101-md** Viavant K./Sipa Press – **101-bg** Boulat P./Cosmos – **101-bd** Haas/Magnum – **102-h** Black Star/Rapho : *Chine (1993)* – **102-b** Sipa Press – **103-h** Riboud M./Magnum – **103-MG** Archive Photos – **103-MD** BUTHAUD/Cosmos – **103-bd** By Alpay/Gamma – **103-b** Kurita K./Gamma – **104-h** Abbas/Magnum – **104-mg** Evrard A./Sipa Press – **104-b** Keystone – **105-h** Dieter/Gamma – **105-mg** Gruyaert H./Magnum – **105-md** Loubat J.M./Gamma – **105-bg** Uzzle/Rapho – **105-b** Renault P./Gamma – **106-h** Setboun/Sipa Press : *Téhéran après la mort de Khomeiny* – **106-m** Capa C./Magnum – **106-b** Alfred/Sipa Press – **107-h** Willis J./Fotogram-Stone – **107-md** Neema F./Sygma – **107-bg** Villard/Sipa Press – **107-bd** Keystone – **108-h** Campbell W./Sygma : *Apartheid en Afrique du Sud* – **108-m** Campion T./Gamma – **109-h** Lounes M./Gamma – **109-mg** Tait S./Gamma – **109-md** Hulton Deutsch/Sipa Press – **109-b** Ascani M./Hoa-Qui – **110-h** F.P.G./Explorer : *Famille américaine des sixties* – **110-b** Keystone Press Agency/Sygma – **111-h** B et F. prod/Pix – **111-mg** Freed L./Magnum – **111-md** Boutin G./Sipa Press – **111-b** Meigneux R./Imapress – **112-h** Boutin G./Sipa Press – **112-m** Archive Photos – **112-b** Lochon F./Sipa Press – **113-h** Bilderberg, Burkard/Studio X – **113-mg** AFP – **113-md** Artacho R./Gamma – **113-b** Henriques B./Magnum – **114-h** Gaillarde R./Gamma : *Drapeau européen* – **114-b** Caratini Ch./Sygma – **115-h** Apesteguy F./Gamma – **115-mg** Nordfoto/Gamma – **115-md** Keystone – **115-b** Keystone – **116-h** Nogues A./Sygma – **116-m** Pedrazzini/Paris-Match – **116-bg** Sipa Press – **116-bd** Bossu R./Sygma – **117-h** Sygma – **117-m** AFP – **117-b** Chech V./Gamma – **118/119** Archives de l'O.N.U. – **119-h** Robert/Sygma

Cartographie : Laurent Blondel

Photogravure : Photochromie, Gentilly – Imprimerie MAME, Tours – Dépôt légal octobre 2000– N° de série éditeur : 19074
Imprimé en France (Printed in France) 652407, octobre 2000

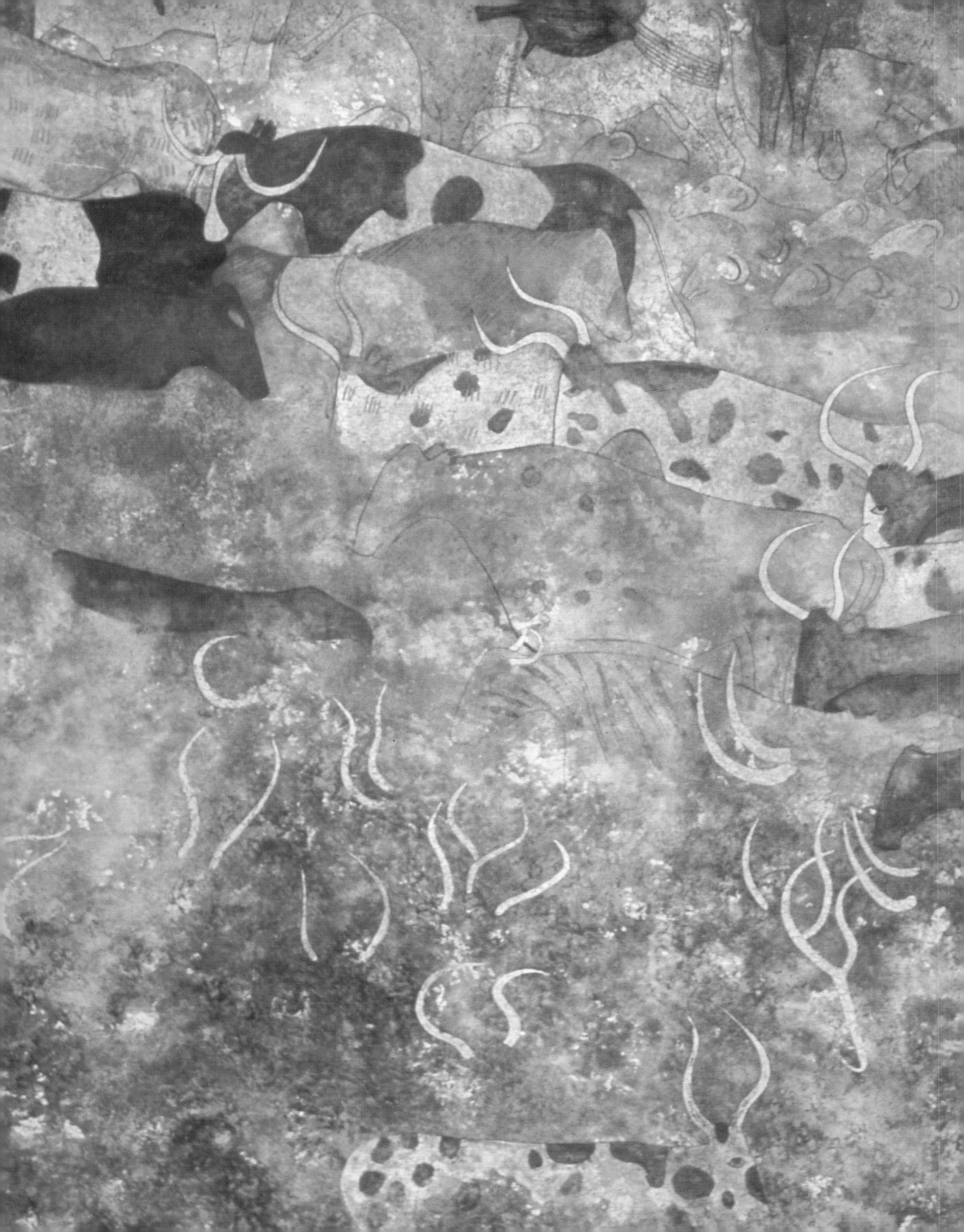